MUSÉE DE CLUNY
MUSÉE NATIONAL DU MOYEN ÂGE

# The Lady
# and the Unicorn

Elisabeth Delahaye

*Director, Musée de Cluny*

*This book is a tribute to the many scholars and amateurs who have studied this famous tapestry and attempted to penetrate its mysteries. First mention should go to the successive curators of the Musée de Cluny, from Edmond Du Sommerard to Alain Erlande-Brandenburg, and from Francis Salet and Geneviève Souchal to Fabienne Joubert and Viviane Huchard, who sought to share with the museum's visitors their passion for its best-known masterpiece. Numerous other specialists have contributed incisive analyses and offered new perspectives on the work, although it has only been possible to mention a few of them in this book, which is intended for a wide audience.*

*My conversations with Nicole Reynaud on style issues and with Marie-Thérèse Gousset regarding the identification of the animals and plants were particularly profitable to this project. The presentation of the plants on pages 80–85 is based on research carried out by the latter in 1998, which unfortunately remains unpublished (see bibliography). I am deeply indebted to both of them.*

*I wish to express my heartfelt gratitude to Elisabeth Clavé, in charge of cultural development at the Musée de Cluny, and to Jean-Christophe Ton-That, head of the museum's documentary resources, not forgetting our interns Marie Ansar, Lucile Douchin and Caroline Vrand, who provided valuable assistance in the preparation of the text, illustrations and bibliography.*

*I extend my thanks to Alexandra Keens, who translated the texts, the book's designers, Frédéric Barrau, Federico Fazzi and Hana Zec of Quartopiano, for their creative and delicate work, and the staff of the Réunion des Musées Nationaux's photographic agency and publishing department, particularly Hugues Charreyron, for their rigorous professionalism. A special mention goes to Laurence Posselle, whose subtle, discerning and careful preparation of the book went far beyond the usual role of an editorial manager.*

*Finally, I should like to express my affectionate gratitude to Francis, Lucile, Timothée and Pauline Delahaye for their unfailing, patient and understanding support.*

# CONTENTS

Like all masterpieces, the *Lady and the Unicorn* tapestry, known as *La Dame à la licorne* in French, has an aura of both familiarity and mystery about it; to the beholder, it seems to encapsulate the era in which it was made, yet is unique. It owes its fame to the quality of its execution, the appeal of the scenes depicted, simple in appearance yet enigmatic; and also to a complex history whose true chronology has become blurred with anecdote and legend.

Much has been written about the tapestry, yet it continues to be the subject of new hypotheses and research. A number of excellent studies of the hangings have been published, along with fresh interpretations purporting to reveal their true meaning, or true story.

The historiography of *The Lady and the Unicorn* reveals a shift in focus in research on the tapestry, no doubt reflecting changing times and new concerns. Historical and geographical issues, primarily those concerning the identity of the work's commissioner and the place where it was woven, dominate in 19th-century publications and, to a very large extent, those of the 20th century. Debate focusing on the style of the tapestries and the artistic milieu in which they were produced arose later in the 20th century, especially from the 1970s and 1980s onwards. In more recent years, there has been renewed interest in the meaning of the work, particularly that of the "sixth piece", and its connections with medieval literature.

The time has come, not for further theories, but, on the contrary, for an updated overview taking account of the most significant discoveries of recent research.

This book aims to provide an introduction to the tapestry and an aid to understanding and appreciating its principal historical, material, conceptual and artistic aspects. It accompanies the reader or visitor in his or her discovery of this fascinating work, and seeks, if not to elucidate every one of its mysteries, at least to answer some questions.

## 1 THE DISCOVERY OF THE HANGING
*A tapestry of anecdote and legend*

*Chateau de Boussac*

*Esquisses des Tapisseries et Boiseries servants à la Décoratio...*

*(N° ... ces Dessins ont été faites sur une échelle de 0.0...*

On 17 July 1882, Edmond Du Sommerard received the six pieces of the *Lady and the Unicorn* tapestry at the Musée de Cluny, which he had directed for almost forty years. This acquisition was the fruit of lengthy and eventful negotiations.

The first mention of the tapestries dates from 1814, in a description of the Château de Boussac – located on the edges of the Berry and Limousin regions in the Creuse département, central France – penned by a local historian, Joseph Joullietton. He mentions that the château houses "old Turkish tapestries which furnished the apartments of the unfortunate Zizim in the Bourganeuf tower". At the time he wrote his text, the château belonged to the Carbonnières family, which acquired it in 1730 through the marriage of François Jean-Baptiste de Carbonnières with Louise de Rilhac, only daughter of Albert de Rilhac, son of François de Rilhac, Baron of Boussac, and Jeanne Armande de La Roche-Aymon.

In 1837, the last heir of the Carbonnières, Pauline, widow of Henri Arnaud de Ribeyreix, sold the château to the town of Boussac. The municipality passed it on to the Creuse département, which, in 1838, made it the headquarters of the sub-prefecture.

In February 1841, the Commission Supérieure des Monuments Historiques expressed concern about the poor state of the Château de Boussac, particularly the "large room containing the tapestries left by Prince Zizine at Bourganeuf where he was imprisoned". In the following July, Prosper Mérimée, inspector of monuments for the Commission, visited the château. In a letter addressed to Ludovic Vitet, president of the Commission, he drew his attention to the presence of six tapestries in the château, expressing concern about what should become of them and suggesting that they be acquired by the Bibliothèque Royale (Royal Library) or placed on the civil list of the king (Louis Philippe). Records made by the architect Morin on 29 September 1842 show tapestries hung amid the wood panelling of two adjoining rooms on the first floor of the château: *Smell*, *Hearing* and *Touch* in the "Large Room", *Taste*, *Sight* and *Mon Seul Désir* in the dining room.

This report appears to have been followed up, for in the minutes of a meeting of the town council on 9 March 1842 mention is made of the sum of 3,000 francs donated by the State, and the council's undertaking to use it to "repair and maintain the town's old château and the tapestries adorning it". An offer of purchase is also alluded to: the town records its "agreement to the handing over of the [tapestries], which are the most remarkable decorations of this old building", but their value is deemed "well above the offer made by M. le Ministre". In several meetings of the town council in the years 1843–1844 mention was made of sums allocated by the State but considered insufficient, and of new requests for subsidies. In 1845–1846, a dispute arose between a former sub-prefect of Boussac and the town: he was accused of having cut up the tapestries hanging in the small room of the sub-prefecture, "which had been temporarily removed from their frames and stored in a cupboard", in order to make a "foot rug".

During this same period, the tapestries aroused the enthusiasm and curiosity of another literary figure, George Sand, thereby contributing to their fame. The *"Bonne Dame"* from nearby Nohant stayed on a number of occasions at Boussac, where she occupied a room neighbouring those containing the tapestries. In her novel *Jeanne* (1844), part of which is set in Boussac, she mentions "those curious enigmatic tapestries". In 1847, she devoted a long article published in *L'Illustration* to the château and its hangings, in which she muses on the subjects of the "eight large panels" and refers to repairs under way at the tapestry-making town of Aubusson – repairs about which we know almost nothing, other than the fact they were probably funded by the town or the sub-prefecture, as the subsidies granted in 1842 by the Commission des Monuments Historiques had been used for the restoration of the château itself. The article is illustrated with drawings by the writer's son, Maurice Sand, of the women depicted in the panels *Touch, Smell* and *Taste*.

Shortly after the sub-prefecture moved into the château and the records made by Morin, the former dining room was partitioned and the three tapestries they contained – *Taste, Sight* and *Mon Seul Désir* – were transported to the town hall, where they appear to have been left in a state of neglect. In 1853, the local erudite Baron Henri Aucapitaine recorded in a "Note on the tapestries of the Château de Boussac" that three "pieces" had been "placed in panels in the sub-prefect's drawing room", that is, at the Château de Boussac, and three others "rolled up in a corner of the town hall at Boussac, where rats and damp have already damaged the edges and would soon cause substantial further deterioration". The short description then given clearly mentions the piece known today as *Mon Seul Désir*: "The third, the finest specimen I know of the genre, shows a woman looking at jewellery in an Oriental tent".

In 1877, the town appears to have come very close to accepting an offer of purchase from a member of the Rothschild family. That same year, the Commission Supérieure des Monuments Historiques – to which the Musée de Cluny had been affiliated since its foundation in 1843 – officially appointed Edmond Du Sommerard, the museum's director, to obtain the sale of the tapestry to the State. In 1878, part of the hangings was sent to the World's Fair at the Trocadéro in Paris, but the town turned down the proposal that the tapestries should be reproduced by the Gobelins factory. On 5 March 1882, the mayor reported to the Boussac town council that the tapestries were "in a such a state of degradation that, to ensure their conservation, it is urgent that they be repaired as soon as possible". He considered "that the repairs they require will entail, according to experts, an expense of twelve thousand francs, that it is materially impossible for the town to incur this expense and that, moreover, there is among the civil buildings no space for the three panels which are stored at the town hall"; he went on to propose to accept the offer from the minister of state education and fine arts and to relinquish the hangings for the sum of 25,500 francs. On 9 June, the Commission des Monuments Historiques decided to grant this sum for the purchase of the six tapestries for the Musée de Cluny; on 14 June, the town council unanimously authorized the mayor to sell them to the State.

When the tapestry entered the Musée de Cluny in July 1882, it was already famous and surrounded in an aura of mystery, It was exhibited shortly afterwards on the first floor of the building designed by Paul Boeswillwald on the west side of the museum buildings, in the room known as the Grande Galerie, opened in 1883.

Its fame had spread through the actions of illustrious figures and because of the long negotiations of which it had been the object. The mystery surrounding the work related mainly to its origins and interpretation.

The crescents featured on the shields, standard flags and banners were at the origin of the legend attributing original ownership of the tapestries to an Eastern prince, Prince Djim or Djem, known as Zizim in the West. This prince had sojourned in Bourganeuf between 1483 and 1488. But this assertion, made in the earliest mentions of the tapestry as well as by the authoritative Commission Supérieure des Monuments Historiques in 1841, was challenged almost immediately, notably by Edmond Du Sommerard. Despite its being unfounded, this hypothesis was advanced frequently throughout the 19th and 20th centuries. The tragic fate of the Ottoman prince Djim (1459–1495) only served to enflame romantic spirits: driven from power by his brother Bayazid (or Bajazet) II in 1482, he sought refuge in Rhodes with the Knights of St John of Jerusalem whose grand master was Pierre d'Aubusson, and was transferred in 1483 to the commanderie tower of this military order, which was located in Bourganeuf. Following negotiations between the king of France and the pope, he was sent to Rome on 10 November 1488, and handed over to Charles VIII in January 1495. He died in mysterious circumstances in Naples in February of the same year, three days after Charles VIII's entrance into the city. It was insinuated that he had been poisoned. But nothing enables us to attribute to this prince, held hostage at Bourganeuf between 1483 and 1488, the creation, or even ownership, of tapestries that were probably not woven until around 1500, and which bear a coat of arms, *Gules a Bend Azure charged with three Crescents Argent Montants,* identified in 1882–1883 as those of family of Lyon lawyers and magistrates, the Le Vistes.

The itinerary of the tapestry from this family to the Carbonnières family, owner of the Château de Boussac between 1730 and 1837, was convincingly charted by Henry Martin (1924-1927). The last male heir of the eldest branch, Antoine II († 1534), had an only daughter, Jeanne, to whom apparently fell both the property of her father and part of that of her cousin Claude, who died childless. Jeanne married Jean IV Robertet, by whom she had a son, Florimond II Robertet (1531-1567), who was secretary of state under Henri II and who died childless, and a daughter, Marie, who married André Guillard (1551), by whom she had four children. The *Lady and the Unicorn* tapestry therefore probably passed to their daughter Catherine, who wed Geoffroy III de Beynac in 1598, then to this couple's son, François, husband of Diane de Hautefort. This last union produced a son, François, who had no children; on François' death, his property went to his mother and then to his mother's sister, Marie de Hautefort, who married François d'Aubusson in 1606. This couple's only heir, Françoise d'Aubusson, married Geoffroi de La Roche-Aymon in 1644. The latter was widowed and remarried in 1660, to Madeleine Des Grillets, herself a widow of Jean de Rilhac, owner of the Château de Boussac, while, on the same day, Jeanne, daughter of Geoffroi de La Roche-Aymon and his first wife, married François de Rilhac, son of Madeleine Des Grillets and her first husband. This is how *The Lady and the Unicorn* would appear to have passed down from the Le Viste family successively to the Guillard, Beynac, d'Aubusson and La Roche-Aymon families, reaching the Château de Boussac, property of the Rilhac family.

When Louise de Rilhac, granddaughter of François de Rilhac and Jeanne de La Roche-Aymon, married François de Carbonnières in 1730, the Château de Boussac and its furnishings passed into the ownership of this last family.

**ABOVE**
Château de Boussac.

**FACING PAGE**
Drawings made by the architect Morin on 29 September 1842 showing the tapestries hung amid the wood panelling of two rooms in the Château de Boussac. Paris, Médiathèque du Patrimoine, 0082/023.

# Chateau de Boussac

*Esquisse des Tapisseries et Boiseries servant à la Décoration de la grande salle.*

*(N° ces Dessins ont été faits sur une échelle de 0.02 p. mètre.)*

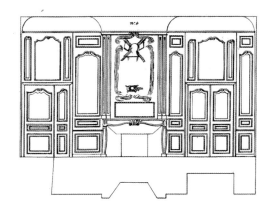

# Chateau de Boussac.

*Esquisses des Tapisseries et Boiseries servant à la Décoration de la salle à manger,*
*Projets de parquet dans cette salle et d'Étagements pour dépôt de la poutre dans la grande salle*

*(N° ces Dessins ont été faits sur une échelle de 0.02 p. mètre).*

## Prosper Mérimée (1803–1870) and *The Lady and the Unicorn*

*Report for Ludovic Vitet*
16 July 1841

"The tapestries of Zizim hang in the sub-prefect's apartment at the Château de Boussac. How they were transported from Bourganeuf to Boussac nobody was able to explain to me. The tower in which Zizim was imprisoned at Bourganeuf still stands but, if my memory serves me correctly, it would have been impossible to hang the tapestries there . . . All six feature a very beautiful woman . . . always placed between a lion and a unicorn . . . There used to be several others at Boussac, finer ones, the mayor tells me, but the former owner of the château . . . cut them up to cover carts and make rugs out of them. Nobody knows what has become of them. Five of the six tapestries are in fine condition. The sixth is a little eaten by rats. They will all share the same fate if we do not remove them from Boussac. Do you not think it would be wise to have them purchased for the Bibliothèque Royale, or, if you prefer, have them bought by the civil list for the king's collection. I prefer the former solution . . . I told the mayor that if he wished to have these hangings repaired in Aubusson we would lose them and that it would cost him a lot of money; and that if they were not so old and tattered, the government may be able to buy them from him".

Quoted in Françoise Bercé, *Naissance des Monuments historiques. La correspondance de Prosper Mérimée avec Ludovic Vitet* (1840–1848), Paris, 1998, pp. 278–279.

## George Sand (1804–1876) and *The Lady and the Unicorn*

*Jeanne*
1844

"The finest decoration of this salon was indisputably those curious tapestries that can still be seen at the Château de Boussac and that are supposed to have been brought from the East by Zizime and have adorned the Bourganeuf tower . . . . These finely worked scenes are masterpieces, and, if I am not mistaken, quite a curious page of history".

Text established, introduced and annotated by Pierre Laforgue, Paris, 2006, p. 154.

"Un coin du Berry
et de la Marche"
1847

"Boussac is an even sharper precipice than Sainte-Sévère. The château . . . is a pretty monument from the middle ages and it contains tapestries that deserve an anti-quarian's attention and research.
I do not know if a local has taken the trouble to find out what these remarkable artefacts represent or symbolise. They have long been left to the rats, fading over the centuries, and are currently undergoing repairs in Aubusson. On eight wide panels that fill two large rooms (occupied by the sub-prefecture), is the portrait of a woman, the same one in each, of course: young, slender, tall, blond, and pretty, clad in eight different attires, all fashions of the late 15th century. . . .

In several of these panels, a pretty young girl, as tall and slim in her high bodice and sheath dress as the chatelaine . . . is shown at her side, handing her a ewer and a golden basin, or, in another, a basket of flowers or jewellery, or, elsewhere, a favourite bird. In one of these scenes, the beautiful woman is sitting facing the viewer, stroking with each hand large white unicorns, which frame her like a coat of arms. . . . the crescent is dotted everywhere on the standards and on the shafts of the blue lances . . . .

"These tapestries are said to have come from the Bourganeuf tower, where they decorated the apartment of the unfortunate Zizime . . . .

"It was long thought that these tapestries were Turkish. They were recently identified as having been produced in Aubusson. . . .

"If I should have . . . just one quarter of an hour to examine these hangings once more, I should find, in the commentary of the details that escape my memory or are unwittingly amplified by it, a solution quite as absurd as one might expect of a professional antiquarian.

"For, after all, the crescent has nothing essentially Turkish about it, and it is found on the escutcheons of a great many noble families in France".

*L'Illustration,* 3 July 1847, vol. IX, no. 227, pp. 275–276.

"My little room, so comfortable in appearance, is, like the others, full of cracks . . . . The drawing room is there, at the end of a small dark corridor . . . . The great fire that was lit in the evening still burns bright. I take advantage of its light to take a leisurely look at the three 15th-century tapestry panels . . . the unicorn was there, not *passant* or *rampant* like some element of heraldry, but on an equal footing with – almost giving its hoof to – a richly and strangely dressed slim lady, who is escorted by a very young girl as flat-chested and slender as her mistress.

This thin blond lady is very mysterious, and looked, at first, to my little girl yesterday, like a fairy. Her very varied outfits are in a strange taste, and I do not know if they were fashionable at the time or a fancy of the artist. I notice an upright *aigrette* [plume] that is simply a bunch of hair gathered in a ribbon, like a paintbrush planted full in the forehead. If we were still under the empire, this novelty should be proposed to the women of the court, who in the latter years would seek so passionately the most desperate of innovations. Everything is dying away, fanciful clothing as well as other flights of fancy. How could we have missed this skyward-brandished ponytail? You have to come to Boussac, the tiniest municipality there can be in France, to discover this new way to please".

Edition introduced by Michelle Perrot, Paris, 2004, p. 64.

*Journal d'un voyageur pendant la guerre*
Boussac, 3 October 1870

*"... there are six tapestries; come, let us pass slowly in front of them. But first of all take a step back and look at them, all together. Are they not tranquil? There is little variety in them. See that blue, oval island in all of them, floating over the soft red background, which is filled with flowers and inhabited by small animals busy with their own activities. There only, in the last panel, the island rises a little, as if it had become lighter. There is always a figure, a woman, wearing different attires, but it is always the same lady. Sometimes, there is beside her a smaller figure, a maidservant, and there are always heraldic creatures: large ones, on the island, which are part of the action. To the left, a lion, and to the right, in light hues, the unicorn; they carry the same banner high above them: three silver moons rising on a blue band on a red field."*

**Rainer Maria Rilke**
*The Notebooks of Malte Laurids Brigge*

In these few finely wrought and precise phrases, all is said: the unity of design that enables us to identify the tapestries as the six pieces of one and the same work; the balanced, sober compositions centring on a kind of platform, or "terrace" – a term used in medieval accounts and inventories – placed over a red ground strewn with flowering plants and animals, the setting for a silent scene in which the principal player is a lady; and, finally, the heraldic character of this hanging, in which a lion and unicorn bear the same coat of arms on each piece.

The order in which the tapestries were described by Rilke *(Taste, Smell, Hearing, Mon Seul Désir, Touch, Sight)* is not the one we have followed in this book: in our presentation of each panel we have respected the hierarchy of the five senses most often observed in the Middle Ages.

**Mon Seul Désir**
The maidservant (detail).

Touch

Taste

Smell

The combination of sobriety and effective composition in each of the *Lady and the Unicorn* tapestries merits emphasis. It is archieved by the "terrace" – Rilke's "island" – placed always over a red ground covered with flowers and animals, and on which, like the elements of a stage set, trees (two or three) and animals bearing the coat of arms (always a lion and a unicorn) frame the lady. She is accompanied in four of the six pieces by a second, smaller female figure, referred to as a "maidservant" by Rilke but whose complex role and elegant dress do not entirely correspond to this over-simplistic description. She might be better decribed as a lady-in-waiting. These figures are not shown in identical fashion but with slight variations from one tapestry to another, playing out on each of them a scene evidently full of meaning. The lady, "never the same exactly, nor exactly different", and her companion are neither portraits nor easily identifiable real-life figures: their solemn poses, sumptuous costumes, abundant jewellery and sophisticated hairstyles give them the air of legendary or allegorical figures.

The identification of five of them as representations of the five senses was first proposed some twenty years before Rilke's text was published, by A.F. Kendrick (1921).

*Hearing*

*Sight*

*Mon Seul Désir*

### Restoration campaigns

The tapestries have come down to us after suffering periods of neglect, mutilation and deterioration, as we have seen. But since their acquisition in 1882, they have also benefited from a number of large-scale and smaller restoration campaigns, the details of which are not always easy to detect in the tapestries in their current state. F. Joubert (1987, pp. 85–92) has given an accurate as possible description of them.

The first restoration carried out, in 1882, consisted simply in filling in the main holes. In the second, done by a lady referred to as "la veuve Plistat" and then the Lameire workshop in 1882–1883, repairs to certain parts of the millefleur grounds in five of the six pieces (excepting *Smell*) were carried out.

The third, in 1889–1892, executed by J. Lavaux at the Gobelins factory under the supervision of Alfred Darcel, restored the lower parts: this woven section is today easily recognizable because the red colour of the grounds, less resistant than that of the old wool threads, has faded into a greyish pink colour.

The fourth restoration, in 1941–1944, carried out by the Brégère workshop, gave the tapestries their present appearance. The lower parts woven in 1889–1892 were retained, except in *Sight*, from which half of the rewoven part was removed, but many old repairs were taken out, large missing or worn areas redone, and many of the facial features were restored.

**The six tapestries**
are reproduced here in the order corresponding to the medieval hierarchy of the senses, from the most material to the most spiritual.

*Touch*

*"What has happened? Why does the little rabbit leap about at the bottom, why can we immediately see that he is leaping? All is so disquieted. The lion has nothing to do. She herself is holding the banner, or is she holding on to it? With her other hand she touches the horn of the unicorn. Is she in mourning? Can mourning remain thus standing? And can mourning dress be as mute as this greenish-black, partially faded velvet?"*

**Rainer Maria Rilke**

On this tapestry, as Rilke notices, the lady is holding the emblazoned banner herself. The lion and the unicorn only carry a shield with scalloped edges, slung over their breasts. The composition, original in this respect, is otherwise one of the most sober of the six. The young woman, standing, her arms spread in two wide gestures, firmly grasps the banner with her right hand and just brushes the horn of the unicorn with her left. The drawing is uneven: the unicorn is similar to that of the other pieces, but the head of the lion is depicted in a different manner to its other representations, with large, bulging eyes, a wide-open mouth and pointed ears – rather like those of the unicorn. Among the animals in the background, there are only two rabbits but a number of birds – falcon, heron, partridge, pheasant –, two monkeys (of two different species), one of which is chained to a roller, and two wild animals with spotted skins, probably a leopard and a cheetah, both wearing collars. The last animal, at the top (between the leopard and the eagle, also spotted and wearing a collar, is more difficult to identify: perhaps a genet, differing slightly from those depicted in *Taste* and *Sight*.

The young woman is clothed not in mourning dress, as Rilke suggests, but in a blue velvet gown whose colour has faded; the gown is lined with ermine and trimmed with goldwork and wide orphreys, ornamental borders decorated with goldwork and precious stones. Her jewellery – a tiara holding back her long, flowing hair, a necklace, and a belt with a long pendant, most of which is made up of assembled chains and disks – all seems to go together.

*Touch*
Wool and silk threads
3.69–3.73 m x 3.52–3.58 m
Inv. Cl. 10835

*Taste*

*"She's feeding a falcon. See her magnificent garment! The bird is perched on her gloved hand, and is moving. She's watching it while putting her hand into a cup brought to her by her servant to give it something. On the right, at the bottom, sitting on her train, is a little silky haired dog, raising its head and hoping there'll be something for him. And – can you see? – a low rose-covered trellis closes off the island at the back. The animals sit or rear up with heraldic pride. Their mistress's coat of arms is printed on their capes fastened with a fine clasp. And flies in the wind."*

**Rainer Maria Rilke**

The bird perched on the lady's gloved hand is not a falcon but a parrot. But the lady is indeed delicately picking a titbit out of the dish held by the maidservant to feed to it. On this tapestry, one of the two largest, the composition is particularly ample and harmonious: the long vertical lines of the trees and banners are linked by transversal lines formed by the bodies of the animals wearing the coat of arms, and enclose within a pyramid the two women forming central group. Behind them, the rose-covered trellis fence carves and rounds out the space, isolating the scene. In front, the monkey mimes the gesture of the lady, bringing a fruit to its mouth. On the ground, a young unicorn, whose horn has not yet grown but recognisable by its little goatee beard and long tail like that of a horse, sits among common and exotic animals: rabbits, dog, lamb, fox, genet, magpie, falcon, monkeys and a lion cub. On the lady's train sits a little pet dog (of the Maltese type), very different from the hunting dogs also depicted on the tapestry. The wide, quiet gestures of the young women contrast with the sharp movements of the lion and the unicorn, who wear armorial capes that seem to float in the wind, and rear up to hold a standard (the lion) and a banner (the unicorn), set atop tall lances. The solemn composition offsets the sumptuous, sophisticated clothing and adornments, revealing details such as apertures tied with laces (the lady's dress, the maidservant's sleeve), orphreys studded with stones and pearls (at the bottom of the lady's dress and the end of her sleeves), and a taste for plant motifs: flowers on the head bands, hair nets and necklaces (alternately gold and blue on the lady's), pomegranates on the lady's belt pendant.

*Taste*
Wool and silk threads
3.74–3.77 m x 4.58–4.66 m
Inv. Cl. 10831

*Smell*

*"Don't we move silently towards the other tapestry, despite ourselves, when we see how much more deeply self-absorbed the lady is? She is weaving a crown, a small round wreath of flowers. Thoughtfully she chooses the colour of the next carnation, in the shallow dish held out to her by the maidservant, while threading in the previous one. Behind her, on a bench, there is a basket of roses that a monkey has found. But it is of no use; this time, it's carnations she needs. The lion has no part here; but on the right, the unicorn understands."*

**Rainer Maria Rilke**

The composition is of the same type as that of *Taste*, but animated to a lesser degree. The lion and the unicorn are rearing, but somewhat stiffly, each wearing a shield slung around its breast. On the one carried by the lion, there is a mistake in the Le Viste arms: the bend azure with three crescents ascending has been replaced with a bend sinister slanting in the opposite direction and bearing three crescents descending.

The maidservant, who was on bended knee in the previous tapestry, stands up very straight here to present her dish of carnations. The lady concentrates on making the crown while, behind her, the monkey sniffs at a rose. The other animals also seem at peace, and only a perfectly harmless lion cub stands among common animals – rabbits, a lamb, a young dog, a heron and a magpie. The dresses of the lady and the maidservant are pinned up to reveal the underskirt. The young woman's cabled necklace matches the belt worn by the lady, who also wears a necklace with a flower motif. A large goldwork clasp and the gown's orphreys studded with stones and pearls heighten the preciousness of her dress. Just above her wrists she wears bracelets in the modern fashion (as opposed to arm bands) studded with stones and pearls. On her head, a short headdress, adorned with rows of pearls and trimmed with precious stones and pearls, which almost entirely covers her hair. The maidservant wears her hair up on the sides of her head in two thick ropes held with ribbons and cut off rather curiously at the top, which hold a short, loose head band in place.

*Smell*
Wool and silk threads
3.67–3.68 m x 3.18–3.22 m
Inv. Cl.10832

# Hearing

 *"Was it not necessary for music to fill this silence? Was it not secretly there already? Gravely and silently adorned, the woman has advanced – so slowly, don't you think? – towards the portable organ, and she plays, standing. The pipes separate her from the servant, who works the bellows on the other side of the instrument. Never have I seen her so beautiful. Her hairstyle is strange indeed: two plaits gathered at the front and tied together on top of her head, splaying out from the knot like a short plume. Looking vexed, the lion endures the sounds with difficulty, containing his desire to yowl. But the unicorn is beautiful, as if quivering in waves."*

**Rainer Maria Rilke**

The composition is tighter here: the armorial flags stand in front of the trees, partly concealing them; only the unicorn's forequarters are visible, somewhat out of proportion and clumsily drawn. This time, the lion holds the banner and the unicorn the standard. They wear neither shield nor cape. The young woman, absorbed in her playing, wears a blue dress with a pinafore cut low over the hips, of a fabric similar to that of the gowns in the other tapestries, decorated with pomegranate motifs and trimmed with borders studded with pearl and precious stones. Rilke notices her original hairstyle, with two plaits on each side of her head raised up into an *aigrette*, or plume, at the top. This time, the lady's hair is contained in a net and covered with a loose band and her companion wears a short veil.

The lady's necklace is set with large precious stones and has little flower-shaped pendants similar to those trimming her hair band. Her companion's necklace is a long chain with a rosette pendant. The musical instrument, a little portable organ, also called a positive organ, set on an Oriental carpet, is decorated with medallions of precious stones and pearls on the side pieces, which are topped by a lion, on one side, and a unicorn on the other – a reminder, if one were needed, of the major role played by these two animals in the tapestry. Again, a peaceful-looking lion cub is depicted among common animals: rabbits, foxes, a dog, a lamb, a falcon and a second bird that resembles a duck, were it not for its spindly, unwebbed feet.

*Hearing*
Wool and silk threads
3.68–3.69 m x 2.90 m
Inv. Cl. 10833

*Sight*

*"Here are more festivities; nobody is invited to them. Expectation has no role in this scene. Everything is there. Everything forever. The lion turns, almost threatening: nobody is permitted to approach. We have never seen her weary. Is she weary? Or is she resting as she holds a heavy object? It resembles a monstrance. But she extends her other arm towards the unicorn and the animal rears up, flattered, and leans on her lap. It is a mirror she is holding. Do you see? She is showing the unicorn its reflection."*

**Rainer Maria Rilke**

The composition, once again sober and efficient, and particularly effective, forms a pyramid whose axis is the seated woman, holding in her right hand a mirror in which the unicorn is looking at its reflection. The central scene is framed by just two trees, with quite low foliage, as if to focus the viewer's gaze. The sole banner is raised above the scene, borne by the lion, who looks away. The young woman, seated here while she stands in the other pieces, strokes the unicorn with her left hand. The unicorn rests its forelegs on the woman's raised dress (made of the pomegranate-motif silk seen previously), revealing the underskirt below. The lady's plume hairstyle is similar to that in *Hearing*. She wears a double cabled necklace with pearl pendants; her belt, without a pendant, unlike the others, is also decorated with pearls. The mirror the young woman holds before the unicorn is a sumptuous piece of goldwork, edged with small cut-out leaf motifs and set with blue stones.

The scene offers a subtle interplay of glances, that of the lady, contemplating the unicorn, and that of the unicorn, observing its own reflection in the mirror. As for the lion, it is looking in a completely different direction. Dotted over the ground and on the terrace, the lion cub and rabbit and the dog and rabbit also seem to be participating in the play of exchanged looks. There is also a genet, some young dogs, a fox and a few other rabbits. *Sight* and *Taste* are the only pieces whose lower parts, rewoven in the late 19th century, features small rabbits among the scattered flowers.

*Sight*
Wool and silk threads
3.11–3,12 m x 3.30 m
Inv. Cl. 10836

# Mon Seul Désir

*"The island has widened. A tent has been erected. Blue damask with a gold flame motif. The animals open it and she advances, simply, in her princely garment. For what are those pearls by her side? The maidservant has opened a small casket, and the lady now takes from it a chain, a marvellous, heavy piece of jewellery, which has been always locked away in the box. The small dog is sitting near her, up on a place made for him, and looks at it. And have you read the inscription at the top of the tent? You can see it says 'A mon seul désir'."*

**Rainer Maria Rilke**

This tapestry differs from the five others in several respects, the principal one being the presence of a blue pavilion tent with a gold flame motif before which the scene unfolds, giving it a particular solemnity. The lion and the unicorn, holding banners, each raise a flap of the tent fabric. At the top is the only inscription in the whole tapestry, and which gives the panel its name. The composition, again forming a pyramid and very wide – the piece is the largest of the six – is organized around the group formed by the lady and the demoiselle, balanced by the small dog – the same as in *Taste* – perched on a stool identical to the one on which the monkey sits in *Smell*. Along with the animals observed in the other tapestries – rabbits, dogs, lamb, monkey, falcon, heron – is a young she-goat.

Is the lady choosing a piece of jewellery, as Rilke suggests, or, on the contrary, is she replacing the necklace, similar in its motif to the one she wears in *Taste*, in the casket? Whatever the case, she has already selected – or kept – her other jewellery, a cabled chain belt and hair ornaments and bracelets (placed at the top of her arms this time, according the etymology of the word, and not above her wrists) with pearl and flower motifs. Here it is the demoiselle who wears her hair in the plume style seen previously. The inscription at the top of the tent has not only given its name to this tapestry but also given rise to much commentary and disputed hypotheses (see page 47).

*Mon Seul Désir*
Wool and silk threads
3.76 –3.77 m x 4.63– 4.73 m

Once fanciful theories based on Prince Zizim's stay in the Limousin region had been dismissed, along with various alchemical and mystical interpretations, a fuller understanding of the tapestry was achieved, notably with A.F. Kendrick's identification in 1921 of five of the six pieces as representations of the five senses.

This interpretation has won the approval of almost all commentators, although conflicting opinions have also been voiced.

Without wishing to discuss every hypothesis here, it is important to note that the manner in the woman is represented, with idealised features and sumptuously adorned to the point of unrealism, does not enable us to recognise her as a real historical figure, however appealing her identification with figures such as Margaret of York (Lanckoronska 1964) or Mary Tudor (Arnaud 1981) may be. Other readings of the tapestry have favoured a more mystical interpretation, such as that of Phyllis Ackerman in 1935 (the Incarnation for *Sight*, the Rosary pour *Taste*, etc.) and Lise Warburg in 1995, which saw the Lady as a representation of the Virgin Mary. Interpretations based on literary parallels have also been made: the illustration of a love story inspired by the principal stages of the hunt of the unicorn, according to medieval bestiaries, suggested by Kristina E. Gourlay in 1997; the allegorical virtues of the *Roman de la Rose*, proposed by Marie-Elisabeth Bruel in 2000 (Frankness for *Taste*, Liberality for *Mon Seul Désir*, etc.). Gottfried Büttner in 1990 saw in the tapestries the illustration of six degrees of the progress of the human soul (childhood for *Smell*, adolescence for *Taste*, adulthood for *Mon Seul Désir*, the practice of meditation for *Sight*, domination of one's surroundings for *Touch*).

However, the explicit character of the scenes, comparison with medieval texts and the parallel with representations of the five senses in the late 15th and early 16th centuries would appear to confirm Kendrick's reading of the tapestry. This interpretation was further corroborated by Carl Nordenfalk (1976; 1985), who showed that while the five senses are more often represented in medieval art in the form of animals – the lynx for Sight, the mole for Hearing, the vulture for Smell, the monkey for Taste, the spider for Touch – their figuration by human figures is recorded as early as the 9th century, and can be found in 13th-century Parisian illuminated texts. This leading specialist of medieval illuminations also emphasised that the first figurations of the five senses in the form of female rather than male figures appear in the late 15th to early 16th centuries. He compared the *Lady and the Unicorn* tapestry to engravings illustrating the *princeps* edition published in Paris in February 1500 of Jodocus Badius's satire on the follies of women, *Stultiferae naves*, a supplement to Sebastian Brandt's *Ship of Fools* (1494). While the allegories in the engravings differ from those of the tapestries in their more material – even trivial – tonality, for example in *Touch*, the similarities with *The Lady and the Unicorn* cannot be disregarded, especially as their models came from the same workshop, as Nordenfalk suggested (1985): the two series were both produced in the same intellectual and artistic milieu. Both have a moral dimension, rooted in medieval tradition, but deliver different messages: the engraving series, introduced by the "Ship of Temptation", illustrates a kind of apologue denouncing the follies caused by the five senses, while the tapestry series, concluded by a sixth piece, conveys an idealized, conciliatory vision.

*Taste*
The maidservant holding the cup from which the lady takes a titbit (detail).

The difficulties begin when we examine this sixth tapestry. The meaning that might be attributed to it depends not only on our understanding of this piece, but also on the meaning of the six tapestries as a whole.

One of the first questions to be addressed is that of the original number of pieces making up the tapestry. The formal, decorative and also conceptual similarities between *Mon Seul Désir* and the five other pieces rule out the former's identification as the only remaining piece of another hanging. We cannot, however, be absolutely certain that *The Lady and the Unicorn* was originally composed of just six pieces: this is the number given by Prosper Mérimée in 1841 and corresponds to the records made by Morin in 1842; but George Sand mentions eight tapestries, in 1847, which she describes in very vague and incomplete terms (see pp. 12–13). It is therefore probable either that her description is based on inaccurate recollections or that she is including two tapestries that are not part of *The Lady and the Unicorn* series. This conclusion is borne out by the mention of another six-piece tapestry entitled *Los Sentidos* ("The Senses"), including a panel entitled *Liberum arbitrium*, purchased in 1539 by Mencía de Mendoza; this work came from the collections of Cardinal Erard de La Marck, prince-bishop of Liège from 1506 to 1538, and must therefore have been produced at around the same time as the tapestry woven for the Le Viste family (Schneebalg-Perelman 1967; Steppe-Delmarcel 1974).

A second question concerns the order in which the pieces should be read. This cannot be dictated by their dimensions because the tapestry's eventful history and current state of preservation prevent us from knowing with any certainty whether the tapestries have retained their original dimensions. The contrary is true for *Touch*, whose composition does not occupy the centre of the piece, which was certainly cut on the left, at the very least. A clue might be found in the number of appearances of the tapestry commissioner's coat of arms; for, as Helmut Nickel noted (1984), these armorial bearings are present once only in *Sight,* twice in *Hearing*, three times in *Touch* et *Mon Seul Désir,* four times in *Taste*, four or five times in *Smell*, depending on whether one counts as one or two appearances the back of the standard flag, partially visible. This remark might afford a central position to *Mon Seul Désir*, which differs from the other pieces in its present larger size and more solemn composition; but it does not shed any light on the meaning of this panel, a key piece to understanding the tapestry as a whole.

It is more tempting to follow the approach recently adopted by Jean-Patrice Boudet (1999; 2000) and Antoine Glaenzer (2002), which looks at the most commonly observed hierarchy of the senses in medieval texts, such as Richard de Fournival's *Bestiaire* and Brunetto Latini's *Li Livres dou trésor*. These order the senses according to a hierarchy defined by the "honourability of their position", that is, their greater or lesser proximity to the soul: the progression, which begins with Touch, is followed by Taste, then Smell, Hearing and finally Sight. It is this order, in reverse, from the nearest to the furthest from the spiritual world, that is followed in the illustrative plates of *Stultiferae naves* published in Paris in 1500. This interpretation has the advantage of placing the sixth piece, *Mon Seul Désir*, naturally at the top of the progression, illustrating a sixth sense, the one closest to the soul or spiritual world. It thus suggests a deeper meaning to this tapestry. Alain Erlande-Brandenburg (1978) was the first to propose interpreting the gesture of the lady not as that of choosing a necklace in the casket, as it had often been described until then, but rather that

FACING PAGE
Master of Anne de Bretagne
and his workshop.
Six engravings illustrating
Jodocus Badius's *Stultiferae*
*naves* (Ship of Women's
Follies), Paris, 1500.
Paris, Bibliothèque Nationale
de France, Rare Book Archives,
Rés. m. Yc. 308.

*Eve and Temptation*

*Ship of the Folly of Sight*

*Ship of the Folly of Hearing*

*Ship of the Folly of Smell*

*Ship of the Folly of Taste*

*Ship of the Folly of Touch*

of replacing the jewellery, noting judiciously that in this panel, unlike the others, the lady wears no necklace. One might even suppose that the light cloth enveloping the necklace contains other items of jewellery that the lady is also preparing to lay aside, in a move towards the simplicity that marks the pre-eminence of the spirit over superficial material pleasures. Comparing the scene of the inscription "Mon seul désir" and that mentioned on one of the pieces of the *Los Sentidos* tapestry from the collections of Cardinal Erard de La Marck, *Liberum arbitrium* ("By [one's] free will"), A. Erlande-Brandenburg proposed seeing in the sixth piece of *The Lady and the Unicorn* not the introduction but the conclusion of the ensemble; this would give it a moral significance borrowed from ancient philosophy: that of the renunciation of the senses illustrated in the five other pieces, and the merit of free will, as in self-control, "mon seul desir" (my desire alone) meaning "my will alone". We might then probe further into this interpretation and ask, which is the sixth sense placed here above the five others? Two hypotheses, both based on currents of thought developed in the late Middle Ages, have been put forward in recent years. Jean-Pierre Jourdan (1996), echoed notably by Alain Jaubert, proposed a comparison with the commentary of Plato's *Symposium* by the Florentine philosopher Marsilio Ficino circa 1468, which had been translated French by Symphorien Champier in the *Livre de vraye amour* published in Lyon in 1503. According to this text, a man has six ways to attain Beauty: through the five senses and also through "understanding", or the mind (*mens* in Latin). The "sixth sense" illustrated in the tapestry might therefore be intelligence, and the inscription "Mon seul désir" might designate beauty (of the soul), one's sole object of desire.

J.-P. Boudet (1999) bases his analysis on the hierarchy of the senses found in medieval bestiaries and in particular on the work of Jean Gerson (1363–1429), chancellor of the university of Paris in the early 15th century, who, in several sermons and in his *Moralité du cœur et des cinq sens* ("Morality of the Heart and the Five Senses") speaks of "six sens, cinq dehors et ung dedans qui est le cuer, lesquelz nous sont baillez à gouverner comme six escoliers" (six senses, five outside and one inside which is the heart, which we obliged to govern like six schoolchildren"). This conception of the five senses and the heart was also explored in a 14th century pastoral manual that was very popular in the following century, the *Doctrinal aux simples gens* ("Doctrinal for Ordinary People"). The sixth sense is thus seen as the heart, the spiritual heart called to govern the five other senses.

This interpretation has the advantage of being based on texts widely distributed in the late 15th century and places the *The Lady and the Unicorn* at the heart of a literary and moral tradition that went back to the beginning of the century, but which found many echoes in the work of thinkers and artists until the early 16th century. It is also that which most easily draws a parallel with the moral conception of the examples drawn from the animal world and conveyed in medieval bestiaries. Philosopher Michel Serres shares this interpretation (1985, pp. 52–53): "An easy, appealing question arises, regarding the sixth tapestry, the only one bearing an inscribed cartouche. Have we five senses or six? . . . A sixth sense is necessary, through which the individual can turn inwards and the body upon itself, a common sense, or internal sense. A sixth island was necessary . . . A tent represents this interior . . ."

We cannot be sure that the meaning of the tapestry is a solely intellectual or moral one, however. Medieval thought accepts multiple meanings that complete each other without

*Taste*
Rose-covered trellis fence
(detail).

being mutually exclusive, and it is possible that these allegories of the senses also had other, more terrestrial and temporal meanings. The heart, as the "sixth sense", was, in the Middle Ages, both the seat of moral life, and the source of free will, and the seat of passion and carnal desire. We should not, therefore, exclude a "courtly" reading of these tapestries, focusing on a female figure and in which the plant decor and flowery grounds, and the predominance of the rose and the carnation, are likened to a garden of love liberally scattered with allusions to desire, exalted in the inscription of the sixth piece.

Similarly, it would be over simplistic to consider the mythical beast that has given its name to the tapestry (the unicorn, the tapestry's French title being "La Dame à la licorne") solely from the angle of its role as an armorial emblem and bearer; the unicorn is an entirely ambivalent fabulous creature, a symbol of chastity but whose principal attribute also has an obvious sexual connotation. As underscored by J.-P. Boudet (2000), the tapestry is highly likely to have more than one meaning: "The heart referred to here is thus both that of courtly love and of Christian morality, the tapestry thus reflecting a double trend in the culture of these great servants of the monarchy: the impregnation of the moral teachings of the clergy, and the celebration of a secular aesthetic".

Should we therefore reject a whole swath of historiography that saw in the tapestry a gift made to a woman – or at least a work executed in honour of a woman? The presence of the plain (i.e. unmodified) coat of arms of one family would appear to exclude the possibility that it may have been made for a married woman, for the coat of arms would then have been partitioned to associate the two families. But what if the wife belonged to a bourgeois family that was not in possession of a coat of arms? And should we totally exclude the hypothesis if not of an engagement or a wedding gift then at least of a commission for one of these occasions, which would serve to display before the bride-to-be the solid moral values as well as the brilliance of the family into which she was entering?

This question is related to the reading of the inscription at the top of the pavilion tent: *A. MON. SEUL. DESIR. I.* If this last letter provides matter for debate, most authors see an I: indeed, a vertical downstroke, alone, can only indicate an I or a J, letters written the same way in the Middle Ages. The curved stroke attached to the letter might suggest a P or an R; but is more likely to be a sign of abbreviation (the stroke would have been fuller and firmer if the draughtsman had wanted to trace one of these two letters). The inscription might therefore be read in two ways: either "A mon seul désir. I" (To my one desire. I), or "A. Mon seul désir. I" (A. My one desire. I.). The letters at each end are separated from the rest of the text by one or two dots, while a group of five dots arranged as a cinquefoil is placed between "mon" and "seul" and between "seul" and "désir", which would appear to support the second hypothesis. It is the former, however, that has been most frequently retained. If the interpretation setting apart the phrase "mon seul désir" from the letters A and I is the correct one, A and I are evidently initials – which may be those of the fiancés or spouses. The words "mon seul désir" would thus appear to refer to the two meanings of the heart, as the sixth sense.

*Mon Seul Désir*
Inscription at the top of the tent
(detail).

## The five senses in medieval literature

Richard de Fournival
*Bestiaire d'amour*
*[The Bestiary of Love],*
mid-13th century

"This is why I say that if I was captivated by Hearing and Sight it is no surprise if I lost my sense and memory. For hearing and seeing are the two windows to the memory, as I said above, and they are the most noble senses of man. For man has five senses: sight, hearing, touch, taste and touch. . . . And I was taken by Smell also, like the unicorn, who falls asleep in the sweet scent of the viriginity of the demoiselle. . . . Love, who is a cunning hunter, placed in my path a young girl whose sweetness sent me to sleep and made me die that death that belongs to Love".

Matthew of Vendôme
(Matheus Vindocinensis),
*Ars versificatoria*
*[The Art of Versification],*
late 13th century

". . . Here blossoms bloom
Sweetly, herbs grow vigorously, trees leaf profusely.
Fruits abound, birds chatter, streams murmur, and
The gentle air warms all. Birds please with song, groves
With shade, breezes with warmth, springs with drink, streams with
Murmuring, the earth with flowers. Pleasant is the stream's
Sound, harmonious the birdsongs, sweet the flowers, cool
The springs, warm the shade. All five senses feast here,
As one may note by noticing all details described.
The streams appeals to the touch, the sweetness to the taste,
The birds to the ear, beauty to the eyes, and fragrance to the nose.
Not one of the four elements is wanting; the earth bears,
The air fosters, the heat quickens, the water nourishes".

Translated with introduction by Aubrey E. Galyon, The Iowa State University Press, Ames, Iowa, 1980, based on the text of the *Ars versificatoria* printed in Edmond Faral, *Les Arts poétiques du XIIe et du XIIIe siècle* (Paris, 1924).

Brunetto Latini
*Li Livres dou tresor*
ca 1266

"And we are ahead of other animals, not by our strength nor common sense but in reason. . . . But the body has five other senses: seeing, hearing, feeling, tasting, touching. And since one precedes the other according to the honourability of its position, in the same manner that one precedes the other in strength . . . But all these things are surmounted by the soul, which is seated in the master fortress of the head and considers through the judgement of its reason what the body does not touch and which does not reach the other senses of the body".

## The heart, sixth sense

**Jean Gerson**
(1363-1429)
*Sermon delivered in Paris*
17 December 1402

"Et parleray des six sens, cinq dehors et ung dedans qui est le cuer, lesquelz nous sont baillez à gouverner comme six escoliers. Premièrement le cuer demande à raison, etc. cuer, bouche, l'eul [œil], tast, flair, oye, De cuer : qui son cuer garde son âme garde."

Jean Gerson, *Œuvres complètes,* Ed. P. Glorieux *et al.,* 1960-1973, vol. VII, 2, p. 826.

*L'Ecole de la conscience*

"Puisqu'ainsy vous plaist, conscience,
je cuer premier mes en sentence
que je suy le plus profitable
le plus gay, le plus honnorable [des sens]
Tresor je suy de connoissance,
de tout art, de toute science.
La fontaine je suy de vie,
de joye et de rennoiserie [...]

Contre toy, cuer, prens la deffense
pour nous cinq lesquels tu tence
... Que saurroyer tu
sans nous cinq, et que vaurroyez-tu
se ne montroit l'oyel les couleurs,
le flair oudeur, je les saveurs,
l'atouchier les affinités..."
*Ibid.,* pp. 6–7.

*L'Ecole de la raison*

"Conscience accuse les cinq
sens comme escoliers à
la maîtresse.
Dame raison ma bonne mère
ie vous nonce nouvelle amère
que j'ay de vos disciples oye,
cuer, langue, œil, tast, flair, oye

Votre fille suis, conscience,
qui accuse les doye en ce.
Tous ont esté, pour verite
en l'escole d'iniquité.
Et le premier ce cuer volage
les aultres maine et fait la rage..."
*Ibid.,* p. 109.

**Charles d'Orléans**
(Charles I de Valois,
Duke of Orléans,
1394–1465)

"De leal cueur, content de joye,
Ma maistresse, mon seul désir,
Plus qu'oncques vous vueil servir,
En quelque place que je soye."

Charles d'Orléans, *Chanson XXVIII,* in *Poésies,* P. Champion (ed.), Paris, 1923, I, pp. 220–221.

**Antoine de Saint-Exupéry**
(1900–1944)

"Goodbye," said the fox. "And now here is my secret, a very simple secret: it is only with the heart that one can see rightly; what is essential is invisible to the eye."

The Little Prince, Paris 1946, p. 72.

**FACING PAGE**
Details from the six tapestries
showing the five senses: Touch,
Taste, Smell, Hearing, Sight,
the "heart".

# 4 THE MAKING OF THE TAPESTRY
*From model to loom*

The art of tapestry-making calls for a series of quite different skills and techniques corresponding to the principal stages of production: the creation of a model in the form of a small sketch, or "*petit patron*", the execution of a full-scale preparatory design, drawn or painted, known as the cartoon, and finally, the weaving.

The first two stages of tapestry-making are connected to the graphic arts and require the skills of a painter or draughtsman; the third is the work of the weaver himself.

The precision of the model and cartoon would be variable. The model might show the design of the whole piece or simply its principal elements. It could even be passed over, when the weaver used figures or decorative elements from an existing cartoon, which he would place over an abstract or repetitive ground. The same model could be used for several pieces of the same tapestry, or in a different hanging altogether. Whatever the case, the painter's or designer's model would necessarily undergo a number of modifications, often a simplification, on its transposition to the cartoon and subsequently during the weaving.

Several aspects characteristic of the development of this art in the late 15th century are to be found in *The Lady and the Unicorn* tapestry. The grounds strewn with flowering plants associate this hanging with a series of pieces executed in the second half of the 15th century and in the very early 16th century known, for this very reason, as millefleurs. The colour of the ground, originally red but faded over the years, and the addition, on the millefleur ground, of a grassy "terrace", also scattered with various flowers but this time in the form of flowerbeds, are, however, more original characteristics. This type of ground marks the high point of a tradition of mural decors

and a fashion for a naturalistic depiction of vegetation that had developed during the Gothic period. It also shows a lack of interest in the representation of space that may appear surprising for this period. Above all, it reflects a desire to rationalize and accelerate the production of the tapestry.

Indeed, to execute this type of tapestry, the weaver had no need of a complete and detailed model. It was sufficient for him to have a drawing of the principal motif, which the cartoonist enlarged to the full scale of the tapestry; he would then reproduce it on a ground composed with plant and animal motifs that were kept at the studio and used from one tapestry to the next. This was probably the case for the *The Lady and the Unicorn:* while the composition of the plants and flowerbeds is carefully varied, the design of each species is always identical. This reproduction of the same design can also be observed among the animals, which sometimes face one way, sometimes the other. In spite of the care taken by the cartoonist, some of his designs are rather clumsy: in *Hearing*, the unicorn's forequarters are somewhat ungraceful and out of proportion; in *Smell*, there is an error on lion's shield (see p. 27) and the lady's hairstyle seems unfinished: the two locks tied with ribbons are abruptly cut off above her head while in other hangings they are gathered up into an *"aigrette"* plume. Moreover, as noted by Fabienne Joubert (1987), in the narrowest pieces and where the terrace is least wide – in *Smell* and, particularly,

*Taste*
The fox (detail).

in *Hearing* – the decorative elements structuring the composition – trees, banners and the animals bearing them – appear tightly clustered, while they are more spaced out in the wider pieces. The cartoonist therefore composed each piece by placing predetermined figures and elements as the fancy took him and, above all, according to his requirements, that is, to fit the dimensions given by tapestry's commissioner. This hanging would appear to have been executed not only for a person but also for a particular place.

The tapestry was personalized by featuring a coat of arms. The number and formal diversity of these heraldic figures and supporting elements, and the highly probable emblematic signification of the two principal animals, the lion and the unicorn, confirm that the hanging was made to a specific order. The painter of the *petit patron* (small preparatory sketch) perhaps not only provided the design of the central group but also that of the other elements, including the lion and the unicorn, although these two figures appear to have been reproduced from several different cartoons. The way in which the central theme of each tapestry is emphasised in the attitude, gesture or even glance of the lion, the monkey and the other animals, suggest that while the cartoonist may have worked with preestablished elements for the principal motifs, he selected and adapted them. The sober, poetic effectiveness of the compositions, elegance of the poses and gestures, and variety and precision of the plant and animal motifs rank *The Lady and the Unicorn* among the most carefully produced and well-executed millefleur tapestries.

*The Lady and the Unicorn*, a relatively heterogeneous ensemble in terms of motifs and style – the millefleur – belongs to a group of works originating in the Paris studios in the latter years of the 15th century. Nicole Reynaud and Geneviève Souchal have identified their connection with the large studio of a painter known as the Master of Anne de Bretagne, who illuminated the *Très Petites Heures d'Anne de Bretagne* (BNF, n. a. lat. 3120). This artist, who worked for the king and queen of France, met with great favour among the high magistrates of Paris and leading ecclesiastics, many of whom, in the late 15th century, belonged to the same families. The manuscripts attributed to him were illuminated in the decade 1490–1500, and his work for engraving was produced between 1490 and 1508, but his models, notably for stained glass and engraving, were distributed, up until the 1520s.

Among the tapestries that have come down to us, a number of those that can be attributed to this master or to his circle are the *petits patrons* of the *Perseus Tapestry* bearing the arms of Charles Guillard (1456–1537), president of the Parlement of Paris (private collection), those of a hanging depicting *Illustrious Women*, of which only fragments remain, notably a figure of Penelope today belonging to the Boston Museum of Fine Arts, and probably also those of the *Life of the Virgin*, intended for the Bayeux cathedral, part of which is kept at the Musée de Cluny. The most famous tapestries from this group are indisputably *The Unicorn Tapestries* at the Metropolitan Museum de New York (The Cloisters collection) and *The Lady and the Unicorn* at the Musée de Cluny.

In *Smell* (left), which is smaller than *Mon Seul Désir* (right), the elements (unicorn, banner, trees) form a tighter composition to occupy less space.

These works are comparable in their balanced compositions, the sweeping, rhythmical gestures of the figures, the serenity of the female figures, whose faces are always oval in shape, and their calm, detached expression; they are also similar in numerous details in the garments, jewellery and hairstyle, such as the two ropes of hair swept up into an *aigrette,* or plume, at the top of the head. Might this last particularity derive from Roman portraits of the Augustinian period, such as those of Livia and Octavia?

To illustrate the theme of the five senses, a highly original one in comparison to other orders received by the studio, despite its connections with medieval literature, the artist had to innovate. Possible comparisons between these tapestries and the signed works by the Master of Anne de Bretagne may therefore be limited.

However, the demoiselle in *Taste* is a repetition, reversed but with only a few modifications, of the design of the Angel of the Annunciation that appears in the manuscript of the *Très Petites Heures* and in many other works attributed to this master or his studio. Above all, the faces, so appealing in their gentle thoughtfulness, despite the simplification caused by the weaving, very probably indicate that the tapestry was based on a model made personally by the master.

The striking similarities between the female figures of *The Lady and the Unicorn,* the young girl in *The Capture of the Unicorn* in the New York hangings, the Boston *Penelope* and the young women in the *Perseus Tapestry* thus confirm that their models have a common origin. Some of the animal motifs, such as the monkey eating a fruit, and the genet, which would appear, like the plume hairstyle, to be a "signature" of the studio and connect *The Lady and the Unicorn* to this studio's significant production of models for engraving. Where this field is concerned, comparison with the plates illustrating the 1500 Paris edition of the *Stultiferae naves* is of particular interest, not only because of the pictorial parallel but also in the similarities in style and in numerous details, such as the design of the mirror in *Sight*.

The question arises as to whether one or several cartoonists from this studio were involved in producing *The Lady and the Unicorn. Touch* differs in its greater overall simplicity and in variants that are without equivalent in the other pieces, notably in the design of the lion and in the original choice and design of the animals featured on the tapestry ground: some appear only in this piece, which favours exotic animals, and many wear a collar, while one of the monkeys is even enchained.

*Sight* (detail)
The unicorn resting its forelegs in the lady's lap. Its position is very close to that of *The Unicorn in Captivity* (facing page), whose preparatory sketches came from the same studio.

***The Unicorn in Captivity***
*The Unicorn Tapestries*, New York,
The Metropolitan Museum
of Art, The Cloisters collection.

Details of the lady in *Taste* and three other tapestries also woven after *petits patrons* by the Master of Anne de Bretagne: *Perseus* (private collection), *The Capture of the Unicorn* (The Unicorn Tapestries, New York, The Metropolitan Museum of Art, The Cloisters collection) and *Penelope* (Boston, Museum of Fine Arts).

Contrary to what has sometimes been said, the garments worn by the two figures of the lady and her companion are indeed fashions of the late 15th century. The long dresses are closely fitted at the chest and tight at the waist, emphasising its shape; the broad rectangular necklines often feature a pointed contour. The sleeves of the dress and pinafore are wide or narrow, short or long; in *Taste*, those of the maidservant's dress are slit up to the shoulder, revealing the light white blouse underneath, with the edges of the aperture held together with small laces. This detail only appeared in France at the very end of the 15th century; it can be seen, for example, in the illustration of the manuscript of Ovid's *Héroïdes* (a French translation of *The Heroides*) in the Bibliothèque Nationale de France, illuminated by Robinet Testard for Louise de Savoie between 1496 and 1498; and in the Magdalen's dress in Jean Poyer's altarpiece *Christ Preaching*, at the church at Censeau (Jura, eastern France), painted circa 1500. This particular detail may, like some of the hairstyles such as the maidservant's hair net in *Taste,* be a fashion imported from northern Italy at the very end of the 15th century (Elsig 2002).

*The Lady and the Unicorn* differs in the care taken in the depiction of these garments. The fabrics are Italian silks, featuring notably the "pomegranate" motif that was in fashion in the late 15th century and early 16th century. The hairstyles have received special attention: the hair is sometimes left loose, sometimes simply held in place with a hair band *(Touch)*, or else covered with a loose band or a veil *(Smell, Taste)*, or gathered inside a net (the maidservant in *Taste*); the hairstyle of two ropes of hair caught up in an *aigrette* or plume, characteristic of the master, is sometimes accompanied with a hair net or band *(Sight* and *Hearing)*. Similar care and variety can be observed in the depiction of the jewellery, which is also characteristic of the period: narrow belts with a long pendant or simply fastened with two medallions studded with pearls and precious stones, circular clasps above the side slit in the dresses, bracelets and, especially, sumptuous chain, cabled or floral-motif necklaces decorated with pearls and stones with pendants made of a single pearl or floral motif. These necklaces derived from types that were widespread from the late 14th century. The necklace disappeared from medieval jewellery only to become popular again from the 1390s onwards in the form of interlinked or cabled chains, or rows of flowers. The fashion lasted throughout the 15th century, as can be seen in the ladies in *Smell* and *Taste* and also in several inventory descriptions – that of Charlotte of Savoy, wife of Louis XI, drawn up in 1483, for example – and a few portraits, such as that of Margaret of York at the Louvre Museum. More rarely depicted, and difficult to distinguish from the orphreys (ornamental borders) decorated with stones and pearls, is the bracelet, worn either high up on the arm or above the wrist, which also appeared or reappeared towards 1390, but does not appear to have been as popular or varied as the other items of jewellery. The pieces featured in *The Lady and the Unicorn* are highly significant in this respect.

While the compositions of *The Lady and the Unicorn* can be attributed to the Master of Anne de Bretagne and the cartoons to the latter's studio, and their place of origin therefore presumed to be Paris, the question of the place the tapestries were actually woven, like that of the millefleur tapestries in general, is much more difficult to resolve. It has been the object of numerous hypotheses and much debate – to little avail, however, for at the time, studios had not yet begun to incorporate their mark into the edge of their tapestries and nothing enabled the identification of the studio or town of production. The idea of "travelling workshops on the banks of the Loire" that emerged in the 19th century from the observation that several of these pieces were found, at the time, in Loire châteaux is completely unfounded. What we can be sure of, however, is that major workshops were active in towns in the north of France and the southern Netherlands: Arras, Lille, Brussels, Tournai, Bruges. The hypothesis that certain of these tapestries may have been woven in Paris, where most of their models were certainly created, is not unfounded, since it was recently established that several important hangings woven in around 1500 were produced in the French capital (Nassieu-Maupas 2004).

Robinet Testard
*Helen Writing to Paris*
Detail from Ovid's *Heroides*.
Western France, 1496–1498.
Paris, Bibliothèque Nationale
de France (BNF), fr. 875 fol. 92.

Jean Bourdichon
*Anne de Bretagne in Prayer*
Detail from *Les Grandes
Heures d'Anne de Bretagne*.
Tours, ca 1503–1508.
Paris, BNF, lat. 9474, fol. 3.

**TOP**
Anonymous
*Margaret of York* (detail).
Southern Netherlands, ca 1477.
Paris, Musée du Louvre.

**The four maidservants**
Details from *Taste, Smell, Hearing*
and *Mon Seul Désir*

**The six ladies**

*Touch*

*Taste*

*Smell*

*Hearing*

*Sight*

*Mon Seul Désir*

## The Master of Anne de Bretagne

The characteristic style of the "Maître d'Anne de Bretagne", active in Paris in 1480–1508, has been described by several art historians, primarily N. Reynaud and G. Souchal (1973). A specialist professional painter, he is known to be the author of mural paintings, illuminated manuscripts, small preparatory sketches and cartoons for stained glass and tapestry, drawings for wood or metal engravings. He has been known by different names, depending on the type of work in question: "Maître d'Anne de Bretagne", after the principal manuscript in which his work is recognizable (a very small book of hours bearing the arms of the queen of France, illuminated in around 1498, Paris, BNF, n. a. lat. 3120), "Maître de la Chasse à la licorne" (Master of the Hunt of the Unicorn) when tapestry is being referred to, a field in which he appears to have dominated the market during the last decade of the 15th century, "Maître de la Rose de la Sainte-Chapelle" or "Maître de Saint Jean-Baptiste" in relation to stained glass, an area in which he was actively involved – his contributions are recognizable in the large edifices constructed at the time: Sainte-Chapelle (a rose bearing the arms and monogram of Charles VIII), Saint-Séverin (chevet, from 1489), Saint-Germain-l'Auxerrois, Saint-Gervais, chapel of the Hôtel de Cluny (circa 1500); and also in churches in Normandy (*Life of St. John the Baptist* at the churches of Conches, Bourg-Achard and Saint-Romain de Rouen).

This master represented a milieu and a type of multi-disciplinary artist that "reflected the multiplicity of tasks that fell to a painter in the late Middle Ages" (Reynaud 1993), and headed a studio that received commissions from a diverse clientele. He belonged to a line of artists that was active in Paris for three or four generations. He himself purchased the stock of the studio of a painter of Northern origin who worked from Paris in 1460–1480, known as the Maître de Coëtivy, whose models he reused in a less expressionistic style and in more sober and more strictly arranged compositions. It is possible that these craftsmen were father and son: Maître de Coëtivy may have been Nicolas or Colin d'Amiens, son of André d'Ypres, himself a painter, and Maître d'Anne de Bretagne may have been his eldest son, Jean, known as Jean d'Ypres, the sworn master of professional painters in Paris in 1504, who died in 1508, a date corresponding exactly to the end of the Master of Anne de Bretagne's activity. It is possible that the genet featured in two pieces of *The Lady and the Unicorn* as well as several engravings from the same studio was a "canting" emblem of this master.

TOP TO BOTTOM
*The Annunciation*
*Très Petites Heures d'Anne de Bretagne*, Paris, ca 1498. Paris, Bibliothèque Nationale de France, n. a. lat. 3120, fol. 28.

*The Annunciation* (detail)
*Heures* printed by Philippe Pigouchet for Simon Vostre, 1498. Paris, Bibliothèque Nationale de France, Rare Book Archives, vellums 2912, fol. 68 r.

*The Temptation of Adam and Eve*
Bible in French printed by Antoine Vérard, Paris, ca 1507. Paris, Bibliothèque Nationale de France, Rare Book Archives, A-273, fol. II.

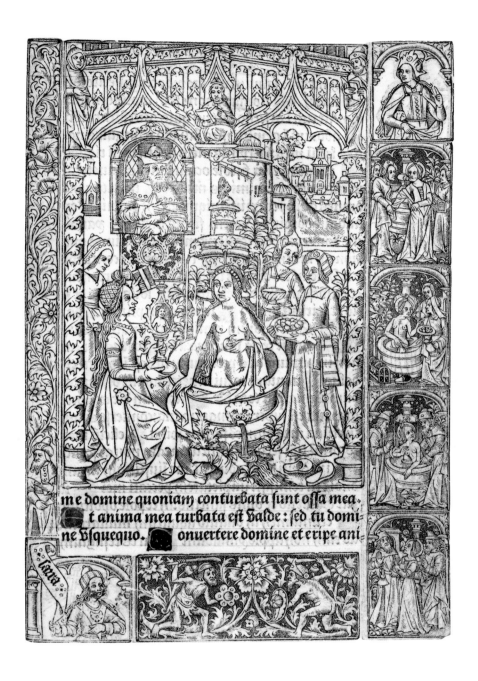

**Bathsheba at Her Bath**
*Heures à l'usage de Rome*
printed by Philippe Pigouchet
1498.

Paris, Bibliothèque Nationale
de France, Rare Book Archives,
vellums 2912, fol. F.7 r.

# 5 FLORA AND FAUNA
*The real and the imaginary*

The flora and fauna in the six pieces of the hanging play multiple and well defined roles. The vegetation is mostly depicted in the form of cut or planted flowers, forming a completely flat decor in which the representation of space is not at all "realist". But the plants also serve as markers in the organization of this space: they give structure to the scene and play a significant role in *Taste* and *Smell*. Similarly, the animals depicted are sometimes reduced in size and dotted among the scattering of decorative flowers, and sometimes, on the contrary, placed in the foreground, bearers of arms or players in the scene.

The sources of this decor have, curiously, been the focus of little research. They can be found in the mural paintings and embroidered hangings adorning the walls of private mansions. Rare examples have been preserved, notably the paintings in the Chambre du Cerf at the Palais des Papes in Avignon, executed under Pope Clement VI (1342–1352), where hunting and fishing scenes are depicted on a ground scattered with little flowers and dotted with bushes. Woven or embroidered pieces decorated with a flower motif, often described in texts, are sometimes reproduced in the accompanying illumination. Examples are the hangings that are reproduced in front of the tabernacle on folio 63 of the *Bible historiale* fr. 9, illuminated in around 1410, kept in the Bibliothèque Nationale de France: with alternate red, blue and green grounds they are strewn with little flowers and feature birds of various species; and those, decorated with clusters of flowers and animals, lining the walls of the hall that was the scene of the tragic "Bal des Ardents" (Ball of the Burning Men), which are reproduced in a manuscript of Froissart's *Chroniques*, illuminated in the third quarter of the 15th century and kept at the British Library (Harley 4380, fol. 1).

The forty or so different species represented with remarkable precision in the *Lady and the* *Unicorn* tapestry are among the common flora of the Middle Ages: wild flowers of the fields or woods – such as daisy, wild pansy, periwinkle (white and blue), Roman hyacinth (white and blue), violet (yellow, white, purplish), lily-of-the-valley (pink and white), speedwell, pimpernel – and garden flowers (jasmine, red and white pinks). Most bloom in spring, and are perhaps an evocation of the May festivities marking the arrival of this season.

As in certain painted or embroidered decors, and in the margins of numerous manuscripts, the flowery grounds of these hangings are dotted with animals. Their number and variety are here rather exceptional among millefleur tapestries. The fauna depicted also reflects the most common animal species in the Middle Ages and, with the exception of the lamb and the goat, and perhaps the magpie, most of them are related to hunting: dog, rabbit, fox, genet, falcon, duck, heron, partridge. Other more exotic animals featured were imported and kept in menageries or tamed and kept as pets: monkey, leopard, lion cub, cheetah; it is therefore not surprising that some should be shown chained up. They are joined in *Taste* by a very young unicorn.

Like the flora, the fauna is not restricted to the decoration of the grounds. Certain animals take part in the allegorical illustration: a monkey

*Sight*
Detail: the rabbit and dog looking at each other.

breathes the scent of a rose in *Smell*; in *Taste*, the lady picks out a titbit (a dragée or piece of sugar) from a dish for a parrot perched on her finger. A small pet dog, of a very different and rarely represented species (a Maltese) to the hunting dogs featured in the grounds, accompanies the lady, sitting on the train of her gown in *Taste* and on a stool in *Mon Seul Désir*. While dogs have long been a symbol of fidelity, the more rarely shown pet dogs appeared in the 15th century in evocations of the marital home, an example being Jan van Eyck's famous *Arnolfini Portrait* (London, National Gallery).

Should the strong presence of animals in this hanging be seen simply as a sign of artistic originality, or should we look for a moral or allegorical meaning? We know that animals played an important role in medieval culture, and were usually invested with a moral signification, manifesting good and evil, or to evoke God or the Devil. However, we should be careful not to over-interpret. As we have seen, the species depicted are generally the most common ones in the late Middle Ages. The monkey, for example, is one of the animals whose moral interpretation was most strongly negative, whether signifying evil, transgression, lustfulness, or ridicule: the monkey eating the fruit *(Taste, Mon Seul Désir)* is perhaps an allusion to original sin; but this animal is extremely common in the medieval repertory, to the point that the term *babouinerie* or *babwinerie* (baboonery) was coined to designate the decors in which it was featured, without it necessarily having a negative connotation. Moreover, the representation in these tapestries of animals in proximity to predator species, the presence of young animals (lion cub, lamb) and their setting among a motif of spring flowers evoke a peaceful and reconciled world, which does not really correspond to the moral vision of the medieval bestiaries.

However, the depiction, in two places, of a heron and a falcon, which seem ready to engage in combat *(Touch, Mon Seul Désir)* seem removed from this peaceful vision. It is possible to see in them an allusion to amorous sparring, these two birds being frequently associated in the Middle Ages and notably in tapestry in courtly contexts, to evoke the man (the falcon) and woman (the heron).

*Hangings with bird and cut-flower motifs.*

The *Bible Historial* translated by Guyart des Moulins, Paris, ca 1410. Paris, Bibliothèque Nationale de France, fr. 9, fol. 63.

The rabbit is the only animal that is present, and most frequently depicted, in all of the pieces (apart from the lion and the unicorn): it appears thirty-four times in five different designs (excluding the parts rewoven in the 19th century). Yet rabbits were not kept as pets in the Middle Ages. They were wild, and hunted as such. But they were know for their fecundity, and the old French word for the animal, *conin* or *conil* (the word *lapin* was introduced at a later date) invites the same word play as the Latin *cuniculus* with the word *con*, designating a woman's genitals. The numerous rabbits scattered over

the hanging were perhaps an allusion to carnal love and symbolic of a wish for fertility.

The lion and the unicorn play highly specific roles. They are not decorative elements, but occupy an important place, always in the foreground, near the lady – excepting the juvenile versions of the animals: a lion cub in four of the six pieces and a young unicorn in *Taste*. These animals bear the coat of arms. They are therefore important signifiers in the hangings, even featured atop the uprights of the organ in *Hearing*. Their roles are not equivalent, however. The lion, whose design and expressions are more

Barthélemy l'Anglais
*Livre des propriétés des choses*
Translated by Jean Corbechon,
illuminated by Perrin Remiet.

Paris, second half of
14th century.
Paris, Bibliothèque Nationale
de France, fr. 216, fol. 283.

Animals shown: lion, bear,
wild boar, stag, crowned
leopard, horse, unicorn,
dromedary, ram.

varied, seems merely to provide a counterpoint to the meaning of each scene; for example, it sticks out its tongue in *Taste*, and looks away in *Sight*. The unicorn is a player, and serves as an identifying element for certain allegories: it is the unicorn that gazes at its reflection in the mirror held by the young woman in *Sight*; in *Touch*, the lady is stroking its horn.

The association of these two animals – which, as A. Erlande-Brandenburg noted in 1978, would appear to justify naming the tapestry "The Lady, the Lion and the Unicorn" – is no novelty. Frequently used in heraldry, it is also found in courtly literature, notably in the 14th century *Roman de la dame à la licorne et du biau chevalier au lion*, in which the knight and the lion deliver the lady and the unicorn, and through which the anonymous author weaves the metaphor of the *"cheene d'amour"* [chain of love], conveyor of desire [Naumann 1993].

The legend according to which only a young girl may capture a unicorn has prompted a wealth of literature and inspired numerous depictions of the capture and kill of the unicorn, including those of the *Unicorn Tapestries* at the Metropolitan Museum de New York (The Cloisters collection). This is not the case in the Musée de Cluny hanging, in which the figures are entirely peaceful; however, the scene in *Sight*, where the unicorn delicately rests its feet on the knees of the lady and approaches her breast to look at itself in the mirror probably derives from this legend.

Bearer of arms, like the lion, in five of the six tapestries, the unicorn figure, depicted in quiet, gentle proximity to the lady, also has its origins in secular poetry and the *Bestiaires d'amour* (love bestiaries), in which it is an ambivalent courtly symbol: an emblem of chastity but also one of eroticism.

Cardinal Charles de Bourbon, archbishop of Lyon († 1488), was in possession of a tapestry depicting the capture of the unicorn. On a decor of Lyon cathedral recorded for Roger de Gaignières, only the lion bears his coat of arms, placed in the foreground in front of a tent similar to the one in *Mon Seul Désir* (Bouchot 1891, no. 1732).

On this hanging, the lion and the unicorn are thus representative of many secular medieval traditions. Moreover, it is highly probable that these animals are "canting" emblems, the former for the commissioner's home city, Lyon, the latter for his patronymic; for one of the qualities attributed to the unicorn was speed, and Viste can be pronounced both "viste" and "vite" (fast).

**Taste**
Detail of the lion.

**Mural painting with the coat of arms and emblems of Charles de Bourbon** (formerly in the cathedral of Lyon.

Drawing heightened with watercolour executed for Roger de Gaignières. Paris, Bibliothèque Nationale de France, Department of Prints, Pc18, fol. 14.

## The lion and the unicorn in the Middle Ages

The lion, king of animals in antiquity (Pliny, Aesop) and later again in the medieval West from turn of the 12th and 13th centuries, a symbol of strength and power and an evocation of Jesus Christ, "the Lion of Judah", a symbol, also, of vigilance and the Resurrection, is one of the most common emblems of royal and princely families and became an arms-bearing figure in the language of heraldry.

The unicorn was one of the mythical creatures passed down to the Middle Ages from antiquity. In his *Natural History*, Pliny the Elder described it as a "licorne" or "unicorn", with the body of a horse and the head of a stag. The horn that gave the creature its name was that of a sea animal, the narwhal.

In the late 13th century on his return from Asia, Marco Polo wrote about the rhinoceros, which he called a "unicorn", but illustrations in his *Book of Marvels* in the 14th and 15th centuries continue to show the animal as a unicorn and not in keeping with the description given by the author of *Description of the World*. According to the *Physiologus* compiled in the 2nd century AD, only a young virgin could capture a unicorn by drawing it to its breast. From the 12th century onwards, the unicorn became a symbol of the Incarnation and, in courtly literature, a symbol of purity and chastity and "captivator" of poets, among whom the trouvère Thibaut of Champagne (Theobald I of Navarre), in one of his most beautiful songs.

**Pliny the Elder**
1st century AD
*Natural History*
Book VIII

"But the most fell and furious beast of all other, is the Licorne or Monoceros: his bodie resembleth an horse, his head a stagge, his feet an Elephant, his taile a bore; he loweth after an hideous manner; one blacke horn he hath in the mids of his forehead, bearing out two cubits in length: by report, this wild beast cannot possibly be caught alive."

First English translation by Philemon Holland, 1601.

**Thibaut IV of Champagne**
*Song-book:*
*"La Capture de la licorne"*
*[The Capture of the Unicorn].*
Paris, ca 1280–1300.
Paris, Bibliothèque Nationale de France, fr. 846, fol. 1

"Like the unicorn, I am lost in wonder
Contemplating the young girl
He delights so in his torment
That he faints upon on the virgin's breast
And at that moment is treacherously killed.
I too have been killed in such a way,
For love and for my lady, in truth:
They hold my heart and I cannot recover it."

**Facing Page**
Detail of the unicorn.

*The animals*

BIRDS

Magpie

TASTE

SMELL

Heron

TOUCH

SMELL

MON SEUL DÉSIR

Falcon

TOUCH

TASTE

HEARING

MON SEUL DÉSIR

Partridge,
pheasant,
duck (?), parrot

TOUCH

TOUCH

HEARING

TASTE

## Dogs

TASTE

SIGHT

HEARING

SMELL

MON SEUL DÉSIR

SIGHT

MON SEUL DÉSIR

TASTE

MON SEUL DÉSIR

## Rabbits

TOUCH

TASTE

SMELL

HEARING

SIGHT

SIGHT

MON SEUL DÉSIR

TASTE

HEARING

SMELL

MON SEUL DÉSIR

TASTE

SMELL

HEARING

HEARING

SIGHT

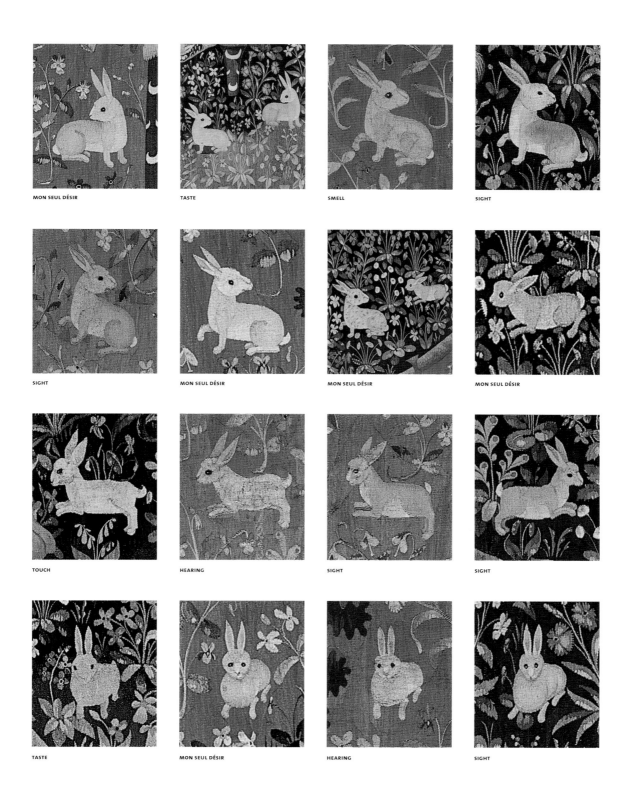

MON SEUL DÉSIR

TASTE

SMELL

SIGHT

SIGHT

MON SEUL DÉSIR

MON SEUL DÉSIR

MON SEUL DÉSIR

TOUCH

HEARING

SIGHT

SIGHT

TASTE

MON SEUL DÉSIR

HEARING

SIGHT

## COMMON ANIMALS

Fox and wolf (?)

TASTE

HEARING

HEARING

SIGHT

Genet

TASTE

SIGHT

TOUCH

Lamb

TASTE

SMELL

HEARING

MON SEUL DÉSIR

Goat

MON SEUL DÉSIR

## Exotic animals

Monkey

TOUCH

TOUCH

TASTE

TASTE

SMELL

MON SEUL DÉSIR

Lion cub

TASTE

SMELL

HEARING

SIGHT

Leopard,
cheetah,
young unicorn

TOUCH

TOUCH

TASTE

# Trees and "millefleurs"

**WILD FLOWERS**

*White columbine*
TOUCH

*Blue columbine*
TOUCH

*European birthwort*
TOUCH

*Spotted arum lily*
SIGHT

*Aster (?)*
SMELL

*Tuberose comfrey*
TOUCH

*Yellow foxglove*
HEARING

*Yellow foxglove*
MON SEUL DÉSIR

*Digitale pourpre*
HEARING

*White swallow-wort*
TASTE

*White swallow-wort*
TASTE

*Large-flowered leopard's-bane*
SMELL

*Large-flowered leopard's-bane*
MON SEUL DÉSIR

*Wild strawberry*
TOUCH

*Wallflower*
SIGHT

*Wallflower*
HEARING

*Field gladiolus*
SIGHT

*Wild hyacinth (?)*
TASTE

*Roman hyacinth (white)*
SIGHT

*Roman hyacinth (blue)*
HEARING

*Roman hyacinth (blue)*
TASTE

*Daffodil*
SMELL

*Dame's rocket/Sweet rocket or Mother-of-the-evening (white)*
SIGHT

*Dame's rocket/Sweet rocket or Mother-of-the-evening (white)*
MON SEUL DÉSIR

*Dame's rocket/Sweet rocket or Mother-of-the-evening (pink)*
SMELL

*Lychnis dioica/Campion (yellow)*
SIGHT

*Lychnis dioica/Campion (yellow)*
SIGHT

*Lychnis dioica/Campion (white)*
MON SEUL DÉSIR

*Lychnis dioica/Campion (white)*
SIGHT

*Oxeye daisy*
HEARING

*Oxeye daisy*
SIGHT

*Oxeye daisy*
TASTE

81

WILD FLOWERS

*Mint*
SMELL

*Mint*
TASTE

*Blue pimpernel*
TASTE

*Blue pimpernel*
SIGHT

*Lily of the valley (white)*
SIGHT

*Lily of the valley (pink)*
MON SEUL DÉSIR

*Daisy*
TASTE

*Daisy*
HEARING

*Wild pansy (white)*
SMELL

*Wild pansy (white)*
HEARING

*Wild pansy (bicoloured)*
TOUCH

*Wild pansy (bicoloured)*
SIGHT

*Periwinkle (white)*
SIGHT

*Periwinkle (white)*
MON SEUL DÉSIR

*Periwinkle (blue)*
SMELL

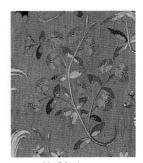

*Periwinkle (blue)*
SIGHT

*Milkwort (white)*
**HEARING**

*Milkwort (blue)*
**TASTE**

*Milkwort (pink)*
**SIGHT**

*Fleabane*
**TASTE**

*Marigold*
**TOUCH**

*Marigold*
**TASTE**

*Speedwell*
**SIGHT**

*Speedwell*
**TASTE**

*Yellow violet*
**TOUCH**

*Yellow violet*
**MON SEUL DÉSIR**

*Sweet violet (purple)*
**HEARING**

*Sweet violet (white)*
**HEARING**

*Wood violet (blue)*
**HEARING**

*Wood violet (white)*
**TASTE**

*Russian violet (blue)*
**HEARING**

*Dog's tooth (?)*
**SIGHT**

**Peaflowers**

*Bladder senna*
SIGHT

*Broad bean*
SMELL

*Broad bean*
TASTE

*Annual vetchling*
HEARING

*Vetchling/sweet pea-False asphodel*
MON SEUL DÉSIR

*Vetch*
TASTE

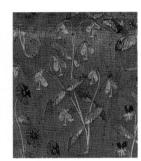

*Vetch*
MON SEUL DÉSIR

*Pea*
SIGHT

**Garden flowers**

*Common jasmine*
MON SEUL DÉSIR

*Common jasmine*
SMELL

*Yellow jasmine*
TASTE

*Yellow jasmine*
SIGHT

*Pink (white)*
TOUCH

*Pink (white)*
MON SEUL DÉSIR

*Pink (red)*
SMELL

*Pink (red)*
HEARING

*Pine*

*Orange*

*Sessile oak*

*Holly*

Gules with a bend azure charged with three crescents argent ascending (three silver moons rising on a blue band on a red field): the coat of arms that has fuelled so much commentary is repeated on each of the six pieces of the hanging.
They are displayed on the shields, banners, standards and armorial capes.
They are emblazoned, like an emblem, along the high lances serving as poles.
In 1882, Edmond Du Sommerard, recognized them as the arms of the Le Viste family.

In these tapestries rich in heraldry, it is also highly probable that the lion and the unicorn are canting emblems for their commissioner's home city (Lyon) and patronymic (Le Viste), as mentioned above.

Such a profusion of heraldic and emblematic symbols and a strong identification with the world of chivalry would appear to reflect a wish to assert a personal and family's identity, typical of those lineages that had acquired wealth and power but lacked noble birth and which sought to attribute themselves with the prerogatives and exterior signs of nobility, starting with a coat of arms.

The social rise of the Le Viste family, which was of Italian origin, is now well documented. The son of Barthélémy, a Lyon clothier who died around 1340, Jean I († 1383) was the first legal man of the family: a doctor of law, he was already in possession of a large fortune. His eldest son, Jean II († 1428), also doctor of law, Chancelier de Bourbon, owned thirty-seven buildings in the city of Lyon. His second son, Barthélemy († 1442), was councillor at the Parlement of Paris. Jean IV (circa 1432–1500), was also councillor at the Parlement of Paris, and spent his career in the service of the Bourbons and subsequently in that of the king – successively Louis XI and Charles VIII. In 1489, he became president of the Court of Aids in Paris, one of the most prestigious offices in the kingdom. This goes to show the political and social benefits that these Lyon families drew from their loyalty to the king of France.

Jean IV was not the only Le Viste to lead a prestigious career in the second half of the 15th century: his uncle Aymé († 1485) was councillor at the Parlement of Paris, and his cousin Aubert († 1493) made his career at the chancellery. Antoine II († 1534), son of Aubert and nephew of Jean IV, succeeded his father as corrector and reporter for the chancellery in 1493; "maître des requêtes" in 1513 and "prévôt des marchands", he was appointed president of the Parlement of Paris in 1523, which was considered the highest rank to which a family could rise.

The matrimonial alliances entered into by the principal members of the family in the 14th and 15th centuries also reveal their social ascension. By obtaining for his son Antoine the hand of Béatrice, only daughter of "chevalier" Mathieu de La Bussière, Jean II acquired for him the seigniory, or lord's domain, of Arcy, and joined the ranks of those wealthy members of the legal profession who united with the local nobility; the latter may have been on the decline on a financial level but it was still in possession of major seigniories.

Jean IV, probably at a relatively advanced age, as seems to have been often the case in this milieu, married Geneviève de Nanterre, only daughter of Mathieu de Nanterre, first president of the Parlement of Paris, thus reinforcing his position in this milieu of magistrates called to higher functions, and also his Parisian anchorage. This alliance with a very old family of the Ile-de-France region around Paris also brought him

*Taste*
Standard with the arms
of the Le Viste family.

a large heritage in terms of land ownership. In 1493, their eldest daughter, Claude, married Geoffroy de Balzac, first "valet de chambre" to King Charles VIII and descendant of a patrician family from the Auvergne that also owned land in the Rhône Valley. Other marriages reflect solidarities within the legal milieu in the second half of the 15th century. Thus, Aubert and his niece Jeanne, second daughter of Jean IV, married sister and brother Jeanne and Thibault Baillet – the latter also a member of the Parlement of Paris, of which he became president in 1484. Both were the children of Jean II Baillet, councillor at the Parlement of Paris and later "maître des requêtes de l'hôtel du roi" and chief reporter at the chancellery († circa 1477). Aubert's son and the daughter, Antoine and Jeanne, married two members of another family of magistrates, Charlotte and Jean Briçonnet. Antoine's only daughter, Jeanne, wedded Jean IV Robertet (1458–1527), treasurer of France under François Ier, "bringing the Robertet family, already so powerful, the better part of the property patiently amassed by the Le Viste family" (Fédou 1964).

The Robertet, Baillet and Briçonnet families evoke another aspect of the role played by the milieu of legal men in the late 15th century, notably those who had embraced an ecclesiastic career: their interest in artistic commissions. Thus, the elder brother of Jeanne and Thibault Baillet, Jean III († 1513), also councillor at the Parlement of Paris, was none other than the bishop of Auxerre, to whom we owe the commission for the tapestry illustrating the *Life of St Stephen*, also acquired by Edmond Du Sommerard for the Musée de Cluny. Guillaume Briçonnet, a close advisor to the king elevated to the rank of cardinal during Charles VIII's stay in Rome in January 1495, was recently recognized as the recipient of one of the most important manuscripts illuminated by the painter Jean Poyer, a book of hours today conserved in Haarlem in the Netherlands (Teylers Museum). For the abbey of Grandmont, of which he was commendatory abbot, he also commissioned the reliquary bust of St Stephen of Muret, today kept in the church of Saint-Sylvestre (Haute-Vienne region), a rare and striking example of late 15th-century gold and silverwork.

It was therefore with a powerful milieu of art lovers that the Le Viste family entered into alliance. Jean II Le Viste had already demonstrated his interest in the arts. Jean IV had major work carried out at the Château d'Arcy, where his coat of arms can notably be seen on a fireplace. In his will, he ordered that a burial chapel be built bearing his coat of arms and decorated with stained glass showing him dressed as a knight. The text also mentions a reliquary of St George paid for partially out of his own pocket, liturgical objects, books and altar ornaments donated by him to the chapel of the Château d'Arcy. Antoine II also had an interest in the arts. In 1532 he commissioned a stained-glass window for the church of Saint-Germain-l'Auxerrois in Paris, which bears his coat of arms.

Is it possible, then, to determine who commissioned *The Lady and the Unicorn*?

The tapestry is the first known representation of the arms of the Le Viste family with tinctures. The stained glass work commissioned by Antoine II shows the same tinctures. However, the arrangement of these colours reveals an anomaly in relation to one of the principal rules of medieval heraldry, namely that two tinctures must not be superposed (in this case, gules and azure). This violation of heraldic rules may correspond to a brisure, or cadency mark, used by the younger branch of the Le Viste family and

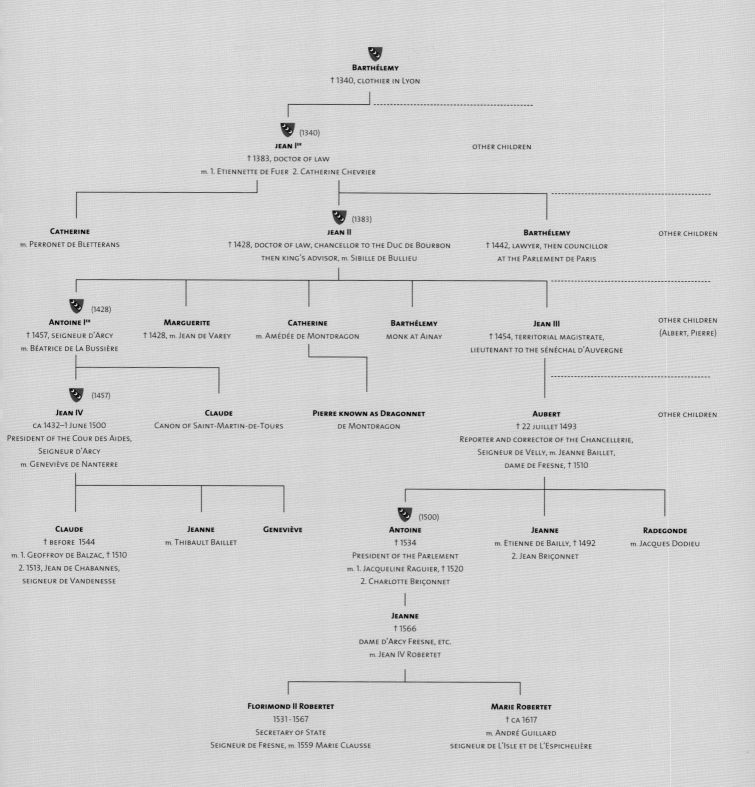

# Genealogy of the Le Viste Family

**Barthélemy**
† 1340, clothier in Lyon

(1340)
**Jean I<sup>er</sup>**
† 1383, doctor of law
m. 1. Etiennette de Fuer  2. Catherine Chevrier

OTHER CHILDREN

**Catherine**
m. Perronet de Bletterans

(1383)
**Jean II**
† 1428, doctor of law, chancellor to the Duc de Bourbon
then king's advisor, m. Sibille de Bullieu

**Barthélemy**
† 1442, lawyer, then councillor
at the Parlement de Paris

OTHER CHILDREN

(1428)
**Antoine I<sup>er</sup>**
† 1457, seigneur d'Arcy
m. Béatrice de La Bussière

**Marguerite**
† 1428, m. Jean de Varey

**Catherine**
m. Amédée de Montdragon

**Barthélemy**
monk at Ainay

**Jean III**
† 1454, territorial magistrate,
lieutenant to the sénéchal d'Auvergne

OTHER CHILDREN
(Albert, Pierre)

(1457)
**Jean IV**
ca 1432–1 June 1500
President of the Cour des Aides,
Seigneur d'Arcy
m. Geneviève de Nanterre

**Claude**
Canon of Saint-Martin-de-Tours

**Pierre known as Dragonnet**
de Montdragon

**Aubert**
† 22 juillet 1493
Reporter and corrector of the Chancellerie,
Seigneur de Velly, m. Jeanne Baillet,
dame de Fresne, † 1510

OTHER CHILDREN

**Claude**
† before 1544
m. 1. Geoffroy de Balzac, † 1510
2. 1513, Jean de Chabannes,
seigneur de Vandenesse

**Jeanne**
m. Thibault Baillet

**Geneviève**

(1500)
**Antoine**
† 1534
President of the Parlement
m. 1. Jacqueline Raguier, † 1520
2. Charlotte Briçonnet

**Jeanne**
m. Etienne de Bailly, † 1492
2. Jean Briçonnet

**Radegonde**
m. Jacques Dodieu

**Jeanne**
† 1566
dame d'Arcy Fresne, etc.
m. Jean IV Robertet

**Florimond II Robertet**
1531-1567
Secretary of State
Seigneur de Fresne, m. 1559 Marie Clausse

**Marie Robertet**
† ca 1617
m. André Guillard
seigneur de L'Isle et de L'Espichelière

Compiled by G. Souchal, 1983

retained by Antoine II since he became head of the family in 1500 (Decu, 2010). However, Jean III, grandfather of Antoine II, also carried arms with a cadency mark, but one in a modification of the bend, which is engrailed on his seal on a document dating from 1446 (de Vaivre, 1984). To imagine that Antoine II changed cadency mark, choosing one that did not conform to heraldic rules and retaining it after becoming head of the family, is a more complex hypothesis than medieval heraldry allows.

What we do know is that Antoine II wore the Le Viste arms as they appear in *The Lady and the Unicorn*. His personality and connections with intellectual and artistic circles in Paris make him a very convincing candidate as commissioner of the tapestry – more so than the ageing Jean IV – while the style and iconography of the tapestries suggest that it was commissioned very close to the year 1500.

There is one last element in the historical enigma. The posthumous inventory of Eléonore de Chabannes, great-niece of Claude Le Viste, drawn up at the Château de Montaigu-le-Blin in the Bourbonnais region in 1595, mentions several hangings with a red ground and a coat of arms with "three crescents", one comprising five pieces with a "sibyl and unicorn" decor, the other seven pieces showing "unicorns and animals". As pointed out by Pierre Verlet and Francis Salet (1960), one must resist the (strong) temptation to identify these tapestries, or at least a part of them, as the *Lady and the Unicorn* hanging; firstly because one would have to explain how these pieces were moved from Montaigu-le-Blin to Boussac, given that the passing of the Le Viste estate into the hands of the Rilhac family, owner in the 17th century of the Château de Boussac, has

been established to a high degree of plausibility; but also because a comparison of the dimensions given in the Montaigu-le-Blin inventory with those of the tapestries kept today at the Musée National du Moyen Âge reveal major differences. Nevertheless, this inventory proves that Claude Le Viste had passed on to her heirs the red-ground unicorn tapestries that she certainly inherited from her father, Jean IV. It thus appears that *The Lady and the Unicorn* was not the only one of its kind. And this lends greater force to the interpretation of the unicorn as a canting emblem of the name of Le Viste. It is possible that the choice of a red ground was related to the colour of the family arms. The possessions of Claude Le Viste may have to be shared between her nephew Charles de Chabannes and her niece Jeanne Le Viste? But it is just as plausible that Antoine II, nephew of Jean IV, following the example of his uncle, may have commissioned a red-ground tapestry featuring a prominent unicorn motif, the canting emblem of their family. This hypothesis corresponds more closely to the different itineraries of the two groups of tapestries bearing the Le Viste arms and emblems, the former mentioned at Montaigu-le-Blin in the late 16th century, the latter reaching Boussac, probably in the middle of the following century. Circumstances such Antoine II's taking up the family plain coat of arms again in 1500, or his engagement with Jacqueline Raguier, (around 1500?), may have prompted the commission for this hanging representing the senses. This hypothesis has the advantage of offering an explanation for the presence of the letters A and I at each end of the inscription on the tent: as the initials of Antoine and Jacqueline, they would have been a discreet allusion associating Antoine's future wife with this fine hanging.

Top of the pavilion

Shield

Standard and armorial cape

Shield with scalloped edges

Banner and armorial cape

While it is quite easy to recognise, in the execution of *The Lady and the Unicorn* as in most medieval tapestries, the successive contributions of skilled artists and craftsmen (the preparatory sketch, the cartoon, the weaving), it is much more difficult to identify the work's designer or designers, responsible for the choice of theme and the treatment of each piece.

The strong presence of the coat of arms and the diverse dimensions of the tapestries indicate, as noted above, not only that they were commissioned but also that they were intended for a specific location. The "Master of Anne de Bretagne", probably Jean d'Ypres, who made the preparatory sketches, created the compositions and provided the designs for the principal figures. But was it the tapestry's commissioner who suggested the theme of the senses and their allegorical treatment, or did he select them among proposals made by the painter, the cartoonist or even the weaver? Should the tapestry's most innovative aspects – the representation of six senses rather than five, and their embodiment in female rather than male figures – be attributed to the client or to the artist? Or might a third person connected to intellectual circles have been involved?

Whether it was Jean IV or Antoine II Le Viste, the person behind the order was one of the new players on the political and artistic scene of the late Middle Ages, who were in the habit of commissioning the most fashionable artists of the capital. The Master of Anne de Bretagne, heir of the traditions of several generations of Parisian painters, adapted to the changing conditions of artistic production by building up a multi-disciplinary studio capable of meeting the most varied demands, both in the traditional arts of illumination and stained glass and the fast-rising art of tapestry, and in the more recent arts of engraving and book illustration.

Through the meeting of these two milieus was born an ensemble that is exceptional in the originality of its design and the quality of its execution. But *The Lady and the Unicorn* tapestry is, above all, unique: in its representation of a poetical world subtly mingling the real and the imaginary; in its balance of composition, pose and gesture amid a mass of spring flowers; in its reconciling not only animals that are natural enemies but also the contradictory tendencies of human nature, the physical world of the senses and that of the spirit. Its resolutely positive vision, faith in man and in a possible reconciliation makes this hanging, which everything seems date very closely to 1500, is perhaps one of the most revealing works of a period in France that saw the shift between two worlds – or simply two moments in history? – one that was a slow maturing process rather than a sudden transformation: those we know today as the Middle Ages and the Renaissance.

*Taste*
The lady (detail).

ACKERMAN, Phyllis, "The Lady and the Unicorn", *Burlington Magazine*, vol. LX, 1935, pp. 35–36.

ARNAUD, André, "La Dame à la Licorne révèle enfin son secret vieux de 5 siècles", *Galerie des Arts*, no. 209, 1981, pp. 21–34.

AUCAPITAINE, Henri, "Notes sur la tapisserie du château de Boussac", *Revue Archéologique*, vol. XIX, 1853, pp. 15–16.

BOUCHOT, Henri, *Bibliothèque nationale. Inventaire des dessins exécutés pour Roger de Gaignières et conservés aux départements des Estampes et des Manuscrits*, Paris, 1891.

BOUDET, Jean-Patrice, "La Dame à la licorne et ses sources médiévales d'inspiration", *Bulletin de la Société nationale des Antiquaires de France*, 1999, pp. 61–78.

BOUDET, Jean-Patrice, "Jean Gerson et la Dame à la licorne", in *Religion et Société urbaine au Moyen Age*, *études offertes à Jean-Louis Biget*, Paris, 2000, pp. 551–553.

BRUEL, Elisabeth, "Les tapisseries de La Dame à la licorne, une représentation des vertus allégoriques du Roman de la Rose", *Gazette des Beaux-Arts*, December 2000, pp. 215–232.

BÜTTNER, Gottfried, *Die Dame mit dem Einhorn, der Teppiche des Musee de Cluny: Bilder der seelischen Entwicklung*, Stuttgart, 1990 [French translation: *La Dame à la Licorne, les tapisseries du musée de Cluny, tableaux d'un chemin spirituel*, Paris, 1996].

BRESC-BAUTIER, G., CRÉPIN-LEBLOND, T., TABURET-DELAHAYE, E., ed., exh. cat. *1500. L'art en France entre Moyen Age et Renaissance*, Paris, Grand-Palais, 2010.

CALLIER, Georges, "Vente des tapisseries de Boussac", *Bulletin monumental*, vol. X, 1882, pp. 567–568.

CALLIER, Georges, *Note sur les tapisseries de Boussac (Creuse)*, Guéret, 1887.

CRICK-KUNTZIGER, Martha, "Un chef-d'œuvre inconnu du "Maître de la Dame à la Licorne"", *Revue belge d'archéologie et d'histoire de l'art*, vol. XXIII, 1934, pp. 3–20.

DECU TEODORESCU, Carmen, "La tenture de La Dame à la licorne. Nouvelle lecture des armoiries", *Bulletin monumental*, 164-4, 2010, pp. 355–367.

DELCOURT, Thierry and TESNIERE, Marie-Hélène, eds. *Bestiaire du Moyen Age. Les animaux dans les manuscrits*, Paris, 2004.

DU SOMMERARD, Edmond, "Tapisseries du XVᵉ siècle provenant du château de Boussac", *Bulletin du Comité des Travaux Historiques et Scientifiques*, 1882, pp. 323–325.

ELSIG, Frédéric, "Un triptyque de Jean Poyet", *Revue de l'Art*, no. 135, 2002, pp. 107–116.

ERLANDE-BRANDENBURG, Alain, "La tenture de la Dame à la licorne conservée au musée de Cluny", *Bulletin de la Société nationale des Antiquaires de France*, 1977, pp. 165–179.

ERLANDE-BRANDENBURG, Alain, *La Dame à la Licorne*, Paris, 1978.

ERLANDE-BRANDENBURG, Alain and ROSE, Caroline, *La Dame à la Licorne*, Paris, 1993.

FEDOU, René, *Les Hommes de loi lyonnais à la fin du Moyen Age*, Paris, 1964.

GLAENZER, Antoine, "La Tenture de la Dame à la licorne, du *bestiaire d'amours*, à l'ordre des tapisseries", *I cinque sensi, Micrologus*, vol. X, 2002, pp. 401–428.

GOURLAY, Kristina E., "La Dame à la Licorne: a Reinterpretation", *Gazette des Beaux-Arts*, September 1997, pp. 47–71.

GOUSSET, Marie-Thérèse, *Essai d'identification des fleurs, arbres et arbustes représentés dans les tapisseries du musée national du Moyen Age*, Paris, 1998, typescript, Paris, musée de Cluny - musée national du Moyen Age, centre de documentation.

GUIFFREY, Jules, *Histoire de la tapisserie depuis le Moyen Age jusqu'à nos jours*, Tours, 1886.

JAUBERT, Alain, *Le Sixième Sens: tenture de la Dame à la licorne (v. 1480-1509)*, film from the "Palettes", Paris, 1997.

JOUBERT, Fabienne, *La Tapisserie médiévale au musée de Cluny*, Paris, 1987, and 3rd ed. revised and expanded by the author in collaboration with Viviane Huchard, Paris, 2002.

JOULLIETTON, Joseph, *Histoire de la Marche et du pays de Combrailles*, 2 vols., Guéret, 1814–1815, new ed. Aubusson, 2002.

JOURDAN, Jean-Pierre, "Le sixième sens et la théologie de l'amour", *Journal des Savants*, 1996, pp. 137–160.

KENDRICK, A. F., "Quelques remarques sur les tapisseries de la Dame à la Licorne du musée de Cluny", *Actes du Congrès d'Histoire de l'Art*, Paris, 1921, vol. III, pp. 662–666.

LANCKORONSKA, Maria, *Wandteppiche für eine Fürstin, die historische Persönlichkeit der Dame mit dem Einhorn*, Frankfurt, 1964.

LORENTZ, Philippe, "La peinture à Paris au XVe siècle: un bilan (1904-2004)", in *Primitifs français. Découvertes et redécouvertes*, exh. cat., ed. by Dominique Thiébaut, Paris, musée du Louvre, 2004, pp. 86–107.

MARTIN, Henry, "La Dame à la licorne", *Mémoires de la Société nationale des Antiquaires de France*, vol. LXXVII, 1924-1927, pp. 137–168.

MONSOUR, Michelle, "The Lady with the Unicorn", *Gazette des Beaux-Arts*, December 1999, pp. 237–254.

NASSIEU-MAUPAS, Audrey, "La *Vie de saint Jean-Baptiste* d'Angers et la production de tapisseries à Paris dans la première moitié du XVIe siècle", *Revue de l'Art*, no. 145, 2004, pp. 41–53.

NAUMANN, Helmut, "Mon seul désir. La Dame à la licorne vor dem Zelt des Aubert Le Viste", *Archivum Heraldicum, Archives héraldiques suisses*, 1993-I, pp. 7–42.

NETTEKOVEN, Ina, *Der Meister der Apokalipsenrose der Sainte-Chapelle und die Pariser Buchkunst um 1500*, Turnhout, 2004.

NICKEL, Helmut, "About the Sequence of the Tapestries in the Hunt of the Unicorn and The Lady with the Unicorn", *The Metropolitan Museum Journal*, 17, 1984, pp. 9–13.

NILSÉN, Anna, "The Lady with the Unicorn. On Earthly Desire and Spiritual Purity", in *Icon to cartoon, A tribute to Sixten Ringbom. Taidehistoriallisia Tutkimuksia, Konsthistorika Studier*, no. 16, 1995, pp. 213–235.

NORDENFALK, Carl, "Les Cinq Sens dans l'art du Moyen Age", *Revue de l'Art*, no. 34, 1976, pp. 25–28.

NORDENFALK, Carl, "Qui a commandé les tapisseries dites de la Dame à la licorne ?", *Revue de l'Art*, no. 55, 1982, pp. 53–56.

NORDENFALK, Carl, "The Five Senses in Late Medieval and Renaissance Art", *Journal of the Warburg and Courtauld Institutes*, vol. XLVIII, 1985, pp. 1–22.

REYNAUD, Nicole, "Un peintre français cartonnier de tapisseries au XVe siècle: Henri de Vulcop", *Revue de l'Art*, no. 22, 1973, pp. 7–21.

REYNAUD, Nicole, "Le Maître des Très Petites Heures d'Anne de Bretagne", in *Les Manuscrits à peintures en France 1440-1520*, exh. cat., ed. by François Avril et Nicole Reynaud, Paris, Bibliothèque nationale de France, 1993, pp. 265–270.

SALET, Francis, and VERLET, Pierre, *La Dame à la licorne*, Paris, 1960.

SCHNEEBALG-PERELMAN, Sophie, "La Dame à la licorne a été tissée à Bruxelles", *Gazette des Beaux-Arts*, November 1967, pp. 253–278.

SERRES, Michel, *Les Cinq Sens*, Paris, 1985.

SOUCHAL, Geneviève, "Un grand peintre français de la fin du XVe siècle: le maître de la Chasse à la Licorne", *Revue de l'Art*, no. 22, 1973, pp. 22–47.

SOUCHAL, Geneviève, "Messeigneurs Le Viste et la Dame à la Licorne", *Bibliothèque de l'Ecole des chartes*, vol. CXLI, 1983, pp. 209–267.

STEPPE, Jan Karel, and DELMARCEL, Guy, "Les tapisseries du cardinal Erard de la Marck, prince-évêque de Liège", *Revue de l'Art*, no. 25, 1974, pp. 35–54.

STERLING, Charles, *La Peinture médiévale à Paris: 1300-1500*, vol. II, Paris, 1990, pp. 333–417.

TUETEY, Alexandre, "Inventaire des robes, étoffes, linges, livres, tapisseries et orfèvreries de Charlotte de Savoie, reine de France", *Bibliothèque de l'Ecole des chartes*, 6th series, I, 1865, pp. 344–366 and 423–442.

VAIVRE, Jean-Bernard de, "Messire Jehan Le Viste, chevalier, seigneur d'Arcy et sa tenture au lion et à la Licorne", *Bulletin monumental*, 1984, pp. 397–434.

WARBURG, Lise, "The Lady and the Unicorn: an iconographical reappraisal", in *Textiles and Tapestries Made or Used in France*, CIETA congress, Paris, 1995, pp. 1–20.

A publication of the
Réunion des Musées
Nationaux – Grand Palais

**Director of Publications**
Henri Bovet

**Head of Book Department**
Marie-Dominique de Teneuille

**Translated from the French by**
Alexandra Keens

**Editorial coordination**
Laurence Posselle

**Graphic design**
Quartopiano

**Production**
Hugues Charreyron

**Picture research**
Agnès Reboul

Texts set in TheAntiqua
and Thesis - TheMix

Photoengraving by
Bussière, Paris

Printed in March 2012
by Aubin (Poitiers, France)

**First registered**
November 2007

**Registered**
March 2012

**ISBN:**
978-2-7118-5035-8
GB 20 5035